DIVORCE GUIDE FOR WASHINGTON
Step-by-step guide to obtaining your own divorce

Mark Patterson, Attorney

Self-Counsel Press Inc.
a subsidiary of
International Self-Counsel Press Ltd.
U.S.A.   Canada

Printed in Canada

First edition: July, 1977
Second edition: December, 1980
Third edition: August, 1983
Fourth edition: May,1987
Fifth edition: February, 1989
Sixth edition: August, 1990; Reprinted: March, 1991
Seventh edition: November, 1991
Eighth edition: April, 1992

Cataloging in Publication Data

Patterson, Mark T.
    Divorce guide for Washington

    (Self-counsel legal series)
    ISBN 0-88908-751-2

1. Divorce — Law and legislation — Washington (State)
— Popular works. 2. Divorce — Law and legislation — Washington (State)
— Forms. I. Title. II. Series.
KFW100.Z9P37 1992   346.79701'66   C92-091207-9

Self-Counsel Press Inc.
1704 N. State Street
Bellingham, Washington 98225
a subsidiary of
International Self-Counsel Press Ltd.
1481 Charlotte Road
North Vancouver, British Columbia
Canada   V7J 1H1

CONTENTS

SAMPLES

NOTICE TO READERS

Laws are constantly changing. Every effort is made to keep this publication as current as possible. However, neither the author nor the publisher can accept any responsibility for changes to the law or practice that occur after the printing of this publication. Please be sure that you have the most recent edition.

Note: The fees quoted in this book are correct at the time of publication. However, fees are subject to change without notice. For current fees, please check with the court registry nearest you.

INTRODUCTION

This book, written by a lawyer, is directed toward filling the general public's need for information. Every citizen should know his or her rights and know how to use the courts to enforce these rights. This book is just one in the Self-Counsel Series, the law and business library for everyone.

The directions and explanations in this book are reduced to a simple step-by-step process to help you understand the divorce proceedings. Although this book does touch on related family problems such as maintenance and custody, we suggest that if you do require further information on family problems you consult *Marriage and Family Law in Washington,* another title in the Self-Counsel Series.

You can obtain your own divorce, as it is the right of every citizen to take his or her own case to court. It will require time and energy on your part, but the ultimate objective of this book is to make lack of money no obstacle to obtaining a divorce. Your efforts could save you as much as $600 in lawyer's fees. Even if you are completely unfamiliar with the operation of the law and the courts, you should be able to obtain a divorce for as little as $100 provided there is no disagreement over custody and you are prepared to represent yourself in court.

However, there are some situations where this book cannot help you and, in these cases, *consultation with a lawyer is absolutely mandatory.* Specifically, if your divorce is contested *for any reason whatsoever,* you will require a lawyer. If you cannot afford a lawyer, you should consult your local legal aid office. According to past statistics, contested divorces account for only 15% of the total number; this book is for the other 85%.

1
CAN I DO MY OWN DIVORCE?

a. DO I NEED A LAWYER?

There *are* cases in which you *cannot* help yourself and will need advice. Even if your divorce is uncontested, there may be procedural complications in your case that will require the services of a lawyer. For example, if you have no idea where your spouse is residing you will have trouble serving the documents on him or her.

As well, there may be maintenance payments, child custody, support and visitation (or parenting functions, as the court now prefers to call them), and matrimonial property matters to be negotiated. If you and your spouse cannot agree on some of these issues, you may want to retain the services of a lawyer to negotiate them.

If you find yourself in these circumstances, you should obtain an estimate of fees for the work to be done. If you are not happy with the cost quoted, feel free to "shop around."

Contrary to popular opinion, most lawyers will give you a quote based on the handling of the case in court, or, for that matter, for any other particular problem for which you feel you need a lawyer. Many people are embarrassed to ask a lawyer for the price of his or her services, especially in family and divorce matters. This can be a costly mistake. DON'T MAKE IT!

The actual court presentation causes the layperson the greatest confusion and fear. If you are uncomfortable at the thought of appearing in court by yourself, you should consider retaining a lawyer for this purpose only.

If you decide to do everything yourself, you should be aware that, while most judges are very cooperative, some are not. Therefore, you should carefully read the section on the court hearing and attend a court session before the same judge prior to your hearing. This will acquaint you with the particular judge's manner of handling divorce cases.

If you do everything yourself, including the court appearance, your divorce could cost you less than $100. You must pay a filing fee to the county clerk. It is now $78, but is changed often by the state legislature, so you should call the county clerk to find out the correct amount. If you must serve copies of the papers on your spouse, the cost of service will probably be between $20 and $30. Once again, you should call the county sheriff or a process server in the county in which your spouse lives for an estimate of cost.

A 1971 United States Supreme Court decision held that a person sincerely seeking a divorce does not have to pay the filing fee if to do so would be a hardship. If you cannot afford the filing fee or cost of service and you want to take advantage of this decision, you should fill in a form entitled In Forma Pauperis, and the court will order the county clerk to file your papers without the fee (see chapter 5).

Even if you have no intention of "doing it yourself," this book should serve as a useful "pre-lawyer" guide to what is happening in your divorce case. It will enable you to be better prepared when seeing your lawyer and to follow your divorce through step by step. This alone should save you unnecessary legal fees.

b. THINK BEFORE YOU START

Think twice about everything that you are doing. Be fully aware of the consequences of your decision to bring a divorce action but particularly what the position of you, your spouse, and your children will be as a result. Seek help from a marriage counselor or other qualified person if you feel there is any chance of a reconciliation.

If you are determined to proceed with a divorce, follow all the suggested procedures very carefully. They are *all* important. Likewise, all forms must be completed with meticulous attention to detail. If you do sloppy work, you could end up paying a lawyer twice as much to correct your mistakes. Be methodical and well prepared at all times.

Be persistent. Do not be afraid to ask questions about the law, even though there may be people who try to discourage your inquiries. Your sincerity and politeness will encourage the proper responses. Contrary to what you might have heard, the divorce courts are quite efficient. Let's keep them that way by not clogging the process with papers and pleadings that are defective.

Although the employees in the county clerk's office cannot give you legal advice, they can tell you how your papers will be processed through their office and how you can have your case placed on the divorce calendar. You can ask them to show you court files of divorce cases in which a person was self-represented. These court files can show you how to be successful in obtaining your own divorce.

If you are well prepared, you should not have to spend more than a few minutes in the courtroom before a judge. If the judge detects carelessness, you could be in for a bad experience, and your lack of knowledge of courtroom procedure will not help the situation.

If you intend to represent yourself in court, you must be especially well prepared. The judge is not there to block your efforts to obtain a divorce, and in most cases, will be helpful. However, the judge does have a specific job to do and must be satisfied that the requirements of the Marriage Dissolution Act have been complied with. This book provides an outline of the types of questions that will be asked. However, you should attend *at least one* court session of uncontested divorces to familiarize yourself with the conduct of a divorce hearing.

If you find yourself getting over your head you will have to make a decision —

(a) to consult a lawyer, or

(b) to drop the action.

The choice is an entirely personal one but, in any event, do not proceed if you do not have a clear understanding of what you are doing. The consequences of errors can be serious and permanent.

c. HOW CAN THIS BOOK HELP ME?

This book is divided into three basic parts. The first part outlines the substantive law of a divorce action. The second part deals with the step-by-step procedure leading up to your court hearing. The third part contains blank forms for you to use to obtain your divorce.

In Washington state, a dissolution of marriage (divorce) may be obtained on the ground that the marriage has "irretrievably broken." While the courts encourage reconciliation, the court is not interested in fault-finding and is more interested in the arrangement you and your spouse have decided upon about your family matters.

You and your spouse must carefully decide what you want the court to do about such matters as child support, custody and visitation (that is, parenting functions), and matrimonial debts and property. You must be sure that what is contained in your divorce papers is exactly the form of relief you want and that you have expressed yourself clearly.

The first part of this book should help you focus on these matters.

The second part of this book is where you will find step-by-step procedures. Directions are set out for the start of your action, through all stages, to the completed divorce.

Each of the steps outlined is important, and each one must be completed before proceeding on to the next. Failure to do this will only result in a great deal of delay and confusion at a later stage.

Do not allow technical words to confuse you. If you encounter terms or phrases foreign to you, look them up in a legal dictionary, which can be found at any library. A glossary of the most common terms is provided in this book. Keep a notebook of such information. It will pay you to research your divorce carefully. Again, it is emphasized that ignorance in the early stages could "snowball" into later difficulties.

Throughout the book you will find illustrations of the forms you will need showing how they should be completed. These are included as *samples only* of commonly used sentences and phrases. Do not copy from them word for word. Use them as guides for the general style and form required when you fill out your forms according to your specific situation.

It is not difficult to draft your own clauses. Put a little work into drafting properly structured sentences and, generally, if they state the truth, they will be acceptable.

While you are following the step-by-step procedure, you will find it necessary to refer constantly to these forms. You may not see the reason for some of them, but they are all necessary for the successful completion of your action.

Blank forms are included at the back of the book for you to tear out and use in the completion of your own divorce. Fill these forms out, using the samples as guides, and following the instructions in the book — and you will be well on your way to successfully filing for divorce.

2

WHAT YOU SHOULD KNOW BEFORE YOU BEGIN

a. BASIS OF DIVORCE

Washington legislation uses the word dissolution rather than divorce. You may apply to the court for a dissolution of your marriage on the sole basis that the marriage has irretrievably broken down. The courts are not interested in assigning fault.

b. CUSTODY

Beginning with all cases filed after January 1, 1988, the state legislature has abolished the use of the words "custody" and "visitation," and has replaced them with the words "parenting functions." Instead of an order or decree granting custody and visitation, each order or decree must contain a "parenting plan" (see Sample #6 in chapter 4).

A parenting plan must contain a decision on whether the major decisions in the child's life will be made jointly, or whether one parent will make the decisions alone (Decision making). It must also contain a division of the time that the child will be physically with each parent including provisions for holidays, vacations, and so forth (Residential provisions). Finally, the law requires that the parenting plan choose a method of settling disputes between the parents. The method may be mediation, counseling, arbitration, or referral to court action (Conflict resolution). In addition to these provisions in which the parties have a choice, there are numerous provisions which must be in every parenting plan.

1. Decision making

The choice you make concerning decision making is about the big decisions such as what school the child will attend, whether non-emergency medical treatment will be given, and what religious training the child will have. The law specifically says that day-to-day decisions will be made by the parent that the child is living with at the particular time that the problem comes up.

2. Residential provisions

The law does not require any particular division of the child's time. It does require that each plan contain a specific decision as to what days the child will spend with each parent. It can provide, for instance, that the child shall reside with the mother during all work days, alternate weekends, and all vacation and holiday time, except those specifically granted to the father, and that the child shall reside with the father every other weekend, every other winter school vacation, the first two weeks of July, and in even-numbered years the following holidays: Christmas Eve, Memorial Day, and Labor Day; and in odd-numbered years, Christmas Day, July 4, and Thanksgiving Day. This is the traditional custody/visitation order. On the other hand, you could go to an equally shared residential time rotating on a month-to-month basis, week-to-week basis, or some other period of time. *Equally shared custody is not favored and can be very harmful to the children. If you decide to do it, you should consult with a lawyer and child psychologist about it before adopting a plan.* The plan may be anywhere in between these examples. There must be some serious danger to the child before a court will eliminate a parent's right to any time of residential care.

3. Conflict resolution

The law requires you to choose a system of deciding disagreements between the parents. The law suggests counseling, mediation, arbitration, or court action. If you have some other agreement, it will probably also be approved. The law also provides an appeal of the decision of the system you have chosen to the superior court. The appeal is to be based on the records kept by the person who decides for you.

c. IF YOU CANNOT AGREE ON A PARENTING PLAN

If you cannot come to an agreement with your spouse on a parenting plan, your only choice is to go to trial (see chapter 4). Before you decide to do that, here are some things you should know about how a judge will decide between your plan and your spouse's plan.

1. Sole decision making

The judge will agree to making one of you the sole decision maker in the following circumstances:

(a) Both parents oppose joint decision making.

(b) One person opposes and the history of the family is that one person has made the decisions regarding the children.

(c) The parents have not demonstrated an ability to cooperate with each other.

(d) The parents live too far apart to communicate with each other quickly enough to make effective decisions.

(e) One parent has abandoned the family for an extended period of time.

(f) One parent has failed or refused, for an extended period of time, to do part or all of the following:

(i) maintain a loving, stable, consistent, and nurturing relationship with the child;

(ii) attend to the daily needs of the child, such as feeding, clothing, physical care and grooming, supervision, health care and day care, and engaging in other activities which are appropriate to the development level of the child and that are within the social and economic circumstances of the particular family;

(iii) attend to adequate education for the child, including remedial or other education essential to the best interests of the child;

(iv) assist the child in developing and maintaining appropriate interpersonal relationships;

(v) exercise appropriate judgment regarding the child's welfare, consistent with the child's developmental level and the family's social and economic circumstances.

(g) A parent has a history of physical, sexual, or emotional abuse of the children.

(h) A parent is guilty of serious acts of domestic violence.

2. Dispute resolution

The court will not require you to adopt any form of dispute resolution other than court action if any of items (e) through (h) above are present.

3. Limitations on residential time

The court may limit or otherwise control the time a parent spends with the child by devices such as supervised visitation if —

(a) any of items (e) through (h) above under sole decision making are present,

(b) there is any long-term emotional or physical problem that interferes with the parenting functions described in

5

item (f) under sole decision making above,

(c) there is a lack of emotional ties between parent and child,

(d) abusive conflict is likely to harm the child's psychological growth, or

(e) one parent is withholding access to the child by the other parent for a long time without good cause.

Warning: After the judge has entered a permanent parenting plan as part of your Decree of Dissolution, it is *very* difficult to change without the agreement of your former spouse. *Be sure to think it through thoroughly and get advice from a child psychologist, attorney, or other person familiar with the problems of divided families before agreeing.*

d. CHILD SUPPORT

A child is entitled to the support of both parents. This right to maintenance cannot be bargained away by the parents through a separate agreement outside of the court. The court will make an order for child support after balancing the needs of the child and the custodial parent with the ability of the non-custodial parent to pay.

The exact amount of child support payments will vary with the circumstances of the parties.

Note: *Child support provisions and parenting plans are revised regularly. To check on changes that might have been introduced since the publication of this book, contact the Office of the Administrator for the Courts, Coordinator for Child Support, 1206 S. Quince, Olympia, 98504 (206) 753-3365.*

The child's basic right to child support payments continues up to the age of majority — 18 years. However, if for health or other justifiable reasons, the child continues to be dependent after the age of 18, the court may order support payments to continue until the child is able to assume independence.

In 1988, the Washington State Legislature adopted a law that requires the courts to use a state-wide child support schedule. The schedule adopted by the legislature is set out in full beginning on page 14. *Before you calculate child support in your case, check with the county clerk to see if the Child Support Table has been changed.*

The first form is the Child Support Table, which sets forth the basic child support obligation to be shared by the parents in proportion to their incomes. The next forms are the Child Support Worksheets. The Worksheets provide for basic child support obligations and include additional factors for consideration. They must be completed in each proceeding. Follow the directions on each sheet to determine the correct amount of support.

The details of child support *must* then be entered on the Child Support Order Summary Report form. If you want to have a support amount either higher or lower than that in the Child Support Table you must put reasons in your Petition and in your Findings of Fact and Conclusions of Law that will convince the judge that support should be either higher or lower than the obligatory amount.

The Worksheets and the Summary Report must be provided to the court if you ask for a temporary order for support on a Motion and Declaration for Temporary Order and the Order of Child Support. They must also be attached to the Decree of Dissolution in every case where there are children involved. Copies of the Worksheets and the Summary Report are included with the forms at the back of this book.

Following the support computation forms are the official instructions that explain how to do the computations. Be sure that you read the instructions carefully.

The Washington State Legislature requires certain language with regard to wage assignment, which you will find in each of the sample forms in this book. This is *not* optional, and in every divorce decree involving minor children this language *must* be used. In addition, the forms in this book use the mandatory language for medical insurance. This may, however, be changed to increase the requirements of the support obligor. It may not be reduced, however, as under Washington law both parties are required to maintain the children as beneficiaries of any employer-supported medical insurance program.

A 1986 act requires all support ordered under dissolution decrees to be paid through the state registry unless the parties agree to direct payment and the court approves it as likely to work. These provisions are set out in the support section of the sample decree. *Be sure that all blanks are filled out correctly.*

e. MAINTENANCE FOR A SPOUSE

The court may award maintenance for the spouse under Section 26.09.090 of the Marriage Dissolution Act. In making such an order, the court may consider the following factors:

(a) Whether any amount has been provided to the spouse as custodian of the children of the marriage, if any

(b) The financial resources and obligations of the party seeking maintenance

(c) The cost of re-educating or retraining the spouse seeking maintenance

(d) The duration of the marriage

(e) The standard of living established during the marriage

(f) The physical and emotional conditions of the spouse seeking maintenance

The court will not take into consideration marital misconduct. The court will weigh the needs of the spouse seeking maintenance against the needs and ability to pay of the spouse from whom maintenance is sought.

Maintenance is, in effect, a means of equalizing the incomes of the spouses or former spouses by requiring one to pay the other a monthly amount of money when the court is satisfied that circumstances warrant such equalization.

Maintenance will rarely be granted for a period of longer than one or two years unless the marriage is long term (more than 15 years). The judicial guidelines further state that combined maintenance and child support should never be more than 50% of the net income of the paying spouse.

A maintenance order (or an order for child support or property disposition) may be modified. Where the spouse paying maintenance can show a substantial change of circumstance, he or she may make a petition for modification to the court.

Forms for applying for modifications are available from the Office of the Administrator for the Courts (see page 6 for address).

Maintenance will be discontinued at the death of the spouse paying or remarriage of the spouse receiving maintenance unless prior written agreements or court orders state otherwise.

Once a maintenance order is made by the court, failure to comply may result in a fine or jail term for contempt of court or garnishment of the non-paying spouse's wages or bank account. Note that the court will not generally make a finding of contempt where failure to make maintenance payments is due to a *real* lack of funds or income on the part of the non-paying spouse.

f. MATRIMONIAL PROPERTY

Under Washington law there are two classes of property: community and separate. Separate property is property owned before marriage, received as a gift or inheritance, or purchased from income earned during a separation. Community property is all property acquired during marriage except gifts or inheritance specifically given to one spouse.

In a divorce action the court has a right to award both classes of property in a way that it determines to be just; however, the normal award is one-half of the community property to each spouse and the separate property to the spouse whose property it is. The division of the property is based on the value of the property, less any amount owed against it.

Factors that lead the court to give more of the property to one spouse than the other are health and earning ability or earning potential. The court usually will not give an unequal division of the property in a marriage of less than 10 to 15 years' duration.

It is important, if you are doing your own divorce, that you and your spouse agree on division of the property. Everything you own must be awarded by the decree or included in your separation agreement. If you and your spouse disagree on division of property or the valuation of the property, you should seek legal counsel.

1. Real property

Matrimonial property matters can be very complicated even if you both agree. If you or your spouse has extensive real estate holdings, you should have a lawyer complete your petition with the correct legal descriptions of the various real estate holdings.

A legal description is the way the court system describes your property. Just as you know your home address, your local court system knows your land by its legal description. If your divorce papers contain incorrect legal descriptions, they will not be legally binding on the property transactions described, and you will have to go through much expense to correct the errors in court.

If you have only your matrimonial home to convey, you may want to do so yourself. In that case, the most accurate way to find out the legal description of your home is to go to the local county courthouse, tell them your address, and ask them to look up your legal description.

You could also employ a title search company (find one in your local Yellow Pages) and pay them a nominal fee to search for the legal description at the county assessor's office.

Sometimes the papers you receive when you purchase your home contain the legal description. Be very careful about using this description unless you have checked it with your county assessor's office, since some papers contain small errors.

You must be sure that the legal description in your petition is accurate. Do not hesitate to seek legal advice if you are the least bit confused about your real estate holdings. In such circumstances, the legal advice you receive may save you time and money. The portion of the decree that awards the real estate *must have a complete and accurate legal description.*

2. Personal property

The division of personal property like furniture and the family car is straightforward. But some personal property may be more difficult to divide. The cash value and death benefits of life insurance policies acquired during the marriage are also subject to the community property laws of Washington. You may need to contact your life insurance agent to determine not only the values of any policies, but the most economical way to convert or retain their values.

Most retirement plans earned during the marriage are property to be divided in the dissolution. These are difficult to value, but where the spouse has been in the plan a number of years, particularly if nearing retirement, the plan may well be the most valuable community asset. If one spouse has considerable time in a plan, an accountant or attorney should be consulted about its valuation and division.

You and your spouse may also have to decide how to divide any joint income tax refund you may receive. This is also considered personal property. You are still a married person during the 90-day reconciliation period following the filing of your Petition for Dissolution, and you can file a joint return if your tax year ends before the divorce decree is filed. Remember to make provision within your petition for the division of any tax refund or debt that may arise from your last jointly filed income tax return. In this way you can avoid any future dispute .

g. SEPARATION AGREEMENTS

Once you separate (or even when you are living together but preparing for separation), you and your spouse may want to agree on certain issues such as maintenance and child support, residential provisions for the children, and the division of joint assets. You and your spouse may put this agreement in writing and sign it. This is called a separation agreement.

A separation agreement is a contract between you and your spouse. The court will give this document the same weight as any other contract; therefore, a separation agreement should be given careful consideration. Ideally, a separation agreement should be drawn up by a lawyer and one party should sign in front of that lawyer, the other party in front of a separate lawyer, so that each receives independent advice about the true legal effect of the agreement. Because a separation agreement should be drawn up by a lawyer specifically for your circumstances, no separation agreement form is included in this book.

You are not required to have a separation agreement. It is sufficient merely to state what you have agreed upon in your Petition for Dissolution.

If one of the parties was forced to sign the separation agreement, or did not receive independent advice, the court may not acknowledge the agreement. Both you and your spouse should be sure that you understand the terms of the separation agreement and that it says exactly what you want it to say. Changing the terms of a separation agreement is a difficult and costly matter, one that will require the advice of a lawyer.

While it is common for a couple to draw up a binding separation agreement without any legal action being taken, Washington law provides a legal route for setting down the terms of your separation. Once you and your spouse agree to the terms of separation and write a separation agreement, you may have it published in the legal notices section of the newspaper and recorded with the county auditor at the courthouse.

Once the separation agreement is both published and recorded, it is binding on both of you. Keep in mind that even a separation agreement that does not follow this procedure can be binding.

There are many advantages to a separation agreement. The drafting of a separation agreement by you and your spouse provides an opportunity to settle your disputes without the cost of litigation. A separation agreement may contain unique clauses that would not have been ordered by the courts, although they may suit your purposes exactly. Therefore, a separation agreement has greater flexibility and potential than a court order.

The provisions of the separation agreement can also be adopted by a judge and made into a formal court order in a divorce action or proceedings in family court, where all the parties are in agreement or where there is no valid reason for having the provisions changed.

If one party attempts to break a separation agreement, the other party should immediately seek the advice of a lawyer, since the issues involved may be numerous and complicated.

Although there is generally no limit to the issues that can be covered in a separation agreement, you and your spouse should give first consideration to the following:

(a) A clause stipulating that neither party will annoy, molest, or interfere with the other

(b) If there are children of the marriage, agreement about the parenting plan (see section **b.** above)

(c) Maintenance and support for the children, including the amount to be paid and the age to which payments will continue (When discussing this matter with your spouse, you should also consider the requirements of the children beyond high school and, in particular, the question of financial assistance to the children should they wish to go to college.)

(d) Dividing community assets, which may include real property such as stocks, bonds, insurance benefits, and joint income tax returns

(e) If the family home is registered in the joint names of husband and wife, agreement on whether —

   (i) the house should be sold and the proceeds of such sale divided between the parties,

   (ii) one party will buy out the other, or

   (iii) one party will continue to live in the home with the children until the family is grown and out on their own (If the wife is to be the main custodian of the children, it is often agreed that she continue to live in the family home with the children. In this case, definite agreement should be reached on payment of mortgages and major repairs, such as a new roof or new furnace, which might be required from time to time. In addition, you should be agreed on when the spouse living in the home should pay the other for his or her share of the equity of the home, the amount of that payment, and the rate of interest to be paid on that amount from the date of the agreement to the date of payment.)

(f) If one spouse agrees to pay maintenance to the other, some provision about the amount to be paid, the times of payments, and under what circumstances the payments will cease (e.g., remarriage or the passage of a given number of years)

(g) If there are debts outstanding prior to the separation of the spouses, a clause stating who is responsible for them (Provision should also be made for indemnifying each party against responsibility for debts incurred by the other after the agreement is signed.)

(h) Release of any interest each of you may have against the estate of the other in the event of death

(i) Provision for determining the effective period of the agreement (i.e., whether it is to be an interim agreement to be terminated upon dissolution of the marriage, or whether it is to continue in effect after a divorce decree has been granted) particularly in regard to property settlement, maintenance, and support for the wife and children

You may want to look at the example of a separation agreement shown in Sample #1. Remember, this is just one example. Your own situation may differ greatly. Under present law the custody provisions must be contained in the parenting plan Form DR 01.0400, which is shown in Sample #6.

h. RESTRAINING ORDERS

Court orders can require one spouse to do something in favor of the other, such as to pay child support, release control of the children, and so forth.

Often, these orders may contain specific provisions requiring a spouse to refrain from acts of violence or harassment aimed at the other. These latter provisions are called restraining orders and are often crucial to the protection of a person from serious danger, especially in the period immediately following separation or a major confrontation.

By either acting alone or through a lawyer, you may make a written motion, accompanied by a declaration, seeking a restraining order. The restraint may be the only relief sought, or it may be combined with other matters, such as a temporary distribution of certain property or temporary child support.

The declaration, filed together with the motion, is a statement of facts which justify and support the request for relief. (See Sample #2.)

Commonly, the two types of relief sought by a motion of this kind are —

(a) immediate relief, such as the restraining provision, which must be granted immediately in order to prevent serious harm or harassment, and

(b) other relief, such as property distribution or child support, which can wait at least a few days.

The motion may ask that the first type of relief be granted immediately on a temporary basis, and that the opposing spouse be required to appear on a certain date (known as the return date) and "show cause" why that order should not be made permanent, pending the final resolution of the case.

In addition, the order will require the opposing spouse to show cause why the other provision should not also be issued as orders at the time.

Because this order, known as an Order to Show Cause, may be granted without notice to the opposing spouse, the courts are limited as to what kind of relief can be ordered immediately. (See Sample #2.)

Only if you, the moving party, are in actual danger, or under threat of danger, will the order take effect immediately, and then it must be worded so that the only provisions that take effect immediately concern the dangerous situation.

The other provision sought in the motion will take effect after your spouse has been served with the Order to Show Cause and has had a minimum of six court days from the time of receiving the order until the return date, at which time he or she may appear with or without a lawyer to argue against the continuation of the restraining provisions or the issuance of any other relief.

The return date must be stated in the order, so your spouse has full notice of it. If he or she fails to appear, the entire relief requested may be granted.

Restraining orders may not be used to change parenting functions from one person to another, to distribute property (other than the necessities of life), to set child support, or to create or enforce a right to visitation. They *may*, however, be sought in the same motion as these other items of relief.

The more common acts that restraining orders may be used to protect against are found in Sample #2 (Form DR 04.0150). Item 1.4 in Sample #11 (Form DR 04.0100), contains a motion for a temporary restraining order.

These acts, and others like them, may be prevented by an order issued without notice to the opposing spouse. The order must then be served upon him or her. (Often, this is done at the very start of proceedings, and the order is served along with the Summons and Petition for Dissolution.)

Many judges are unwilling to restrict access to the children or family home without notice to the opposing party. This relief should be sought only where the danger of physical harm is readily apparent.

After the order has been served it is enforceable by the police. By law, violation of a court order may be punished by the court with a short jail term and/or a fine, if the restraining order provisions are followed by the following notice in capital letters:

NOTICE: VIOLATION OF THE ABOVE PROVISIONS OF THIS ORDER WITH ACTUAL NOTICE OF THEIR TERMS IS A CRIMINAL OFFENSE UNDER CHAPTER 26.09 R.C.W., AND WILL SUBJECT THE VIOLATOR TO ARREST. RCW 26.09.060(5).

If you have a restraining order, it should be taken to the county sheriff to be recorded on the computer. The sheriff does this without fee. *It is necessary to do this or the police may not enforce your order.*

i. OTHER TEMPORARY ORDERS

Frequently, other orders are obtained that are maintained until the final order (decree) of dissolution. You may ask for anything that seems necessary. Typical temporary orders deal with residential arrangements for the children, visitation and support, use of the family home or car, etc. See Sample #11 for the form that these orders would take.

j. TAX ASPECTS OF SEPARATION AND DIVORCE

If you make payments for the support of your spouse, these payments may be deducted from your gross income to compute your taxable income, provided that the following conditions are met:

(a) The payments must be made directly to your spouse or to a third party with your spouse's consent and for his or her benefit (e.g., to the mortgage company).

(b) The payments must be for the benefit of the spouse personally — not labeled as "child support."

(c) If the amount of the maintenance exceeds $10,000.00 per year ($833.33 per month), it must continue for a minimum of three years to be a deduction.

(d) The payments must be made according to a written separation agreement or an order of the court.

For tax purposes, your spouse will have to include in his or her income all payments that you properly deduct. If the payments do not meet all of the above conditions, however, they are not deductible and, therefore, your spouse need pay no tax on them.

The most important thing you should remember about the tax consequences of separation agreements, and even court orders calling for payments of money from one spouse or ex-spouse to the other, is that certain kinds of payments are *taxable income* to the recipient, and others are not.

Since all parents, whether married or divorced, are required by law to contribute to the support of their children, there is no tax deduction or credit for such payments.

But separate maintenance (formerly known as alimony) is different. Payments made according to a written separation agreement or court decree that labels them as maintenance are deductible from the gross income of the spouse making the payments and are taxable for the recipient spouse.

Hence, it is in the best interests of the spouse *making* the payments to have them called separate maintenance so they will be a tax savings; likewise, it is in the best interests of the spouse *receiving* the payments to have them labeled child support, so they will not be taxable income.

A compromise can be reached by dividing the total payment into two *specified* amounts, one under each category.

These are just some considerations to take into account in phrasing a separation agreement or, for that matter, in deciding how a court order or Decree of Dissolution should best be worded. The considerations can become quite complicated, and there are certain situations in which you would be best advised to seek the counsel of a lawyer.

The point to be stressed is that a separation agreement can clear up a number of tax difficulties before they arise, and can create a savings for both parties if done correctly.

Currently, the law gives the dependency exemption for the children to the person who has the children in his or her care for the greater part of each year without regard to the amount of financial support given by the other. The physical custodian may give up the exemption by signing a form to be attached to the tax return of the non-custodian that says the custodian is not claiming the exemption. This form can be obtained from your nearest Internal Revenue Service office.

If your decree provides for maintenance or if you are selling real estate as part of your agreement to dissolve your marriage, talk to an attorney or a CPA about the tax consequences of these decisions. Also, if one of you will have a lien against the family home as part of the agreement, talk to a lawyer about the form of the lien as a protection against bankruptcy of the spouse who retains the real estate.

If the family home is to be sold as part of the agreement, consult an accountant regarding the tax impact of that decision. Depending on the timing of the sale, you may save substantial money.

WASHINGTON STATE CHILD SUPPORT TABLE
MONTHLY BASIC SUPPORT OBLIGATION PER CHILD

KEY: A = AGE 0-11; B = AGE 12-18										
COMBINED MONTHLY NET INCOME	ONE CHILD FAMILY		TWO CHILDREN FAMILY		THREE CHILDREN FAMILY		FOUR CHILDREN FAMILY		FIVE CHILDREN FAMILY	
	A	B	A	B	A	B	A	B	A	B
600	133	164	103	127	86	106	73	90	63	78
700	155	191	120	148	100	124	85	105	74	91
800	177	218	137	170	115	142	97	120	84	104
900	199	246	154	191	129	159	109	135	95	118
1000	220	272	171	211	143	177	121	149	105	130
1100	242	299	188	232	157	194	133	164	116	143
1200	264	326	205	253	171	211	144	179	126	156
1300	285	352	221	274	185	228	156	193	136	168
1400	307	379	238	294	199	246	168	208	147	181
1500	327	404	254	313	212	262	179	221	156	193
1600	347	428	269	333	225	278	190	235	166	205
1700	367	453	285	352	238	294	201	248	175	217
1800	387	478	300	371	251	310	212	262	185	228
1900	407	503	316	390	264	326	223	275	194	240
2000	427	527	331	409	277	342	234	289	204	254
2100	447	552	347	429	289	358	245	303	213	264
2200	467	577	362	448	302	374	256	316	223	276
2300	487	601	378	467	315	390	267	330	233	288
2400	506	626	393	486	328	406	278	343	242	299
2500	526	650	408	505	341	421	288	356	251	311
2600	534	661	416	513	346	428	293	362	256	316
2700	542	670	421	520	351	435	298	368	259	321
2800	549	679	427	527	356	440	301	372	262	324
2900	556	686	431	533	360	445	305	376	266	328
3000	561	693	436	538	364	449	308	380	268	331
3100	566	699	439	543	367	453	310	383	270	334
3200	569	704	442	546	369	457	312	386	272	336
3300	573	708	445	549	371	459	314	388	273	339
3400	574	710	446	551	372	460	315	389	274	340
3500	575	711	447	552	373	461	316	390	275	341
3600	577	712	448	553	374	462	317	391	276	342
3700	578	713	449	554	375	463	318	392	277	343
3800	581	719	452	558	377	466	319	394	278	344
3900	596	736	463	572	386	477	326	404	284	352
4000	609	753	473	584	395	488	334	413	291	360

KEY: A = AGE 0-11; B = AGE 12-18										
COMBINED MONTHLY NET INCOME	ONE CHILD FAMILY		TWO CHILDREN FAMILY		THREE CHILDREN FAMILY		FOUR CHILDREN FAMILY		FIVE CHILDREN FAMILY	
4100	623	770	484	598	404	500	341	422	298	368
4200	638	788	495	611	413	511	350	431	305	377
4300	651	805	506	625	422	522	357	441	311	385
4400	664	821	516	637	431	532	364	449	317	392
4500	677	836	525	649	438	542	371	458	323	400
4600	689	851	535	661	446	552	377	467	329	407
4700	701	866	545	673	455	562	384	475	335	414
4800	713	882	554	685	463	572	391	483	341	422
4900	726	897	564	697	470	581	398	491	347	429
5000	738	912	574	708	479	592	404	500	353	437
5100	751	928	584	720	487	602	411	509	359	443
5200	763	943	593	732	494	611	418	517	365	451
5300	776	959	602	744	503	621	425	525	371	458
5400	788	974	612	756	511	632	432	533	377	466
5500	800	989	622	768	518	641	439	542	383	473
5600	812	1004	632	779	527	651	446	551	389	480
5700	825	1019	641	791	535	661	452	559	395	488
5800	837	1035	650	803	543	671	459	567	401	495
5900	850	1050	660	815	551	681	466	575	407	502
6000	862	1065	670	827	559	691	473	584	413	509
6100	875	1081	680	839	567	701	479	593	418	517
6200	887	1096	689	851	575	710	486	601	424	524
6300	899	1112	699	863	583	721	493	609	430	532
6400	911	1127	709	875	591	731	500	617	436	539
6500	924	1142	718	887	599	740	506	626	442	546
6600	936	1157	728	899	607	750	513	635	448	554
6700	949	1172	737	911	615	761	520	643	454	561
6800	961	1188	747	923	623	770	527	651	460	568
6900	974	1203	757	935	631	780	533	659	466	575
7000	986	1218	767	946	639	790	540	668	472	583

WASHINGTON STATE CHILD SUPPORT SCHEDULE WORKSHEETS

Washington State Child Support Schedule
Worksheets

Mother _____   Father _____

County _____   Superior Court Case Number _____

Children and Ages:			
Part I: Basic Child Support Obligation (See Instructions, Page 5)			
1. Gross Monthly Income		Father	Mother
a. Wages and Salaries		$	$
b. Interest and Dividend Income		$	$
c. Business Income		$	$
d. Spousal Maintenance Received		$	$
e. Other Income		$	$
f. Total Gross Monthly Income (add lines 1a through 1e)		$	$
2. Monthly Deductions from Gross Income			
a. Income Taxes		$	$
b. FICA/Self-Employment Taxes		$	$
c. State Industrial Insurance Deductions		$	$
d. *Mandatory* Union/Professional Dues		$	$
e. Pension Plan Payments		$	$
f. Spousal Maintenance Paid		$	$
g. Normal Business Expenses		$	$
h. Total Deductions from Gross Income (add lines 2a through 2g)		$	$
3. Monthly Net Income (line 1f minus line 2h)		$	$
4. Combined Monthly Net Income (add father's and mother's monthly net incomes from line 3)		$	
5. Basic Child Support Obligation (enter total amount in box ⟶) Child #1 _____ Child #3 _____ Child #2 _____ Child #4 _____		$	
6. Proportional Share of Income (each parent's net income from line 3 divided by line 4)		.	.
7. Each Parent's Basic Child Support Obligation (multiply each number on line 6 by line 5)		$	$
Part II: Health Care, Day Care, and Special Child Rearing Expenses (See Instructions, Page 7)			
8. Health Care Expenses			
a. Monthly Health Insurance Premiums Paid for Child(ren)		$	$
b. Uninsured Monthly Health Care Expenses Paid for Child(ren)		$	$
c. Total Monthly Health Care Expenses (line 8a plus line 8b)		$	$
d. Combined Monthly Health Care Expenses (add father's and mother's totals from line 8c)		$	
e. Maximum Ordinary Monthly Health Care (multiply line 5 times .05)		$	
f. Extraordinary Monthly Health Care Expenses (line 8d minus line 8e, if "0" or negative, enter "0")		$	
Continue to Next Page			

WORKSHEET — Continued

Part II: Health Care, Day Care, and Special Child Rearing Expenses (cont.)		
9. Day Care and Special Child Rearing Expenses	Father	Mother
a. Day Care Expenses	$	$
b. Education Expenses	$	$
c. Long Distance Transportation Expenses	$	$
d. Other Special Expenses (describe)	$	$
	$	$
	$	$
e. Total Day Care and Special Expenses (add lines 9a through 9d)	$	$
10. Combined Monthly Total of Day Care and Special Expenses (add father's and mother's total day care and special expenses from line 9e)	$	
11. Total Extraordinary Health Care, Day Care, and Special Expenses (line 8f plus line 10)	$	
12. Each Parent's Obligation for Extraordinary Health Care, Day Care, and Special Expenses (multiply each number on line 6 by line 11)	$	$
Part III: Standard Calculation Child Support Obligation		
13. Standard Calculation Support Obligation (line 7 plus line 12)	$	$
Part IV: Child Support Credits (See Instructions, Page 8)		
14. Child Support Credits		
a. Monthly Health Care Expenses Credit	$	$
b. Day Care and Special Expenses Credit	$	$
c. Other Ordinary Expense Credit (describe)		
	$	$
d. Total Support Credits (add lines 14a through 14c)	$	$
Part V: Net Support Obligation/Presumptive Transfer Payment (See Instructions, Page 8)		
15. Net Support Obligation (line 13 minus line 14d)	$	$
Part VI: Additional Factors for Consideration (See Instructions, Page 8)		
16. Household Assets (List the estimated present value of all major household assets.)	Father's Household	Mother's Household
a. Real Estate	$	$
b. Stocks and Bonds	$	$
c. Vehicles	$	$
d. Boats	$	$
e. Pensions/IRAs/Bank Accounts	$	$
f. Cash	$	$
g. Insurance Plans	$	$
h. Other (describe)	$	$
	$	$
	$	$
	$	$
Continue to Next Page		

WORKSHEET — Continued

	Father's Household	Mother's Household
17. Household Debt (List liens against household assets, extraordinary debt.)		
	$	$
	$	$
	$	$
	$	$
	$	$
	$	$
18. Other Household Income		
a. Income Of Current Spouse (if not the other parent of this action) Name	$	$
Name	$	$
b. Income Of Other Adults In Household Name	$	$
Name	$	$
c. Income Of Children (if considered extraordinary) Name	$	$
Name	$	$
d. Income From Child Support Name	$	$
Name	$	$
e. Income From Assistance Programs Program	$	$
Program	$	$
f. Other Income (describe)	$	$
	$	$
19. Non-Recurring Income (describe)		
	$	$
	$	$
20. Child Support Paid For Other Children		
Name/age:	$	$
Name/age:	$	$
21. Other Children Living In Each Household (First names and ages)		

Continue to Next Page

WORKSHEET — Continued

22. Other Factors For Consideration

(blank lines for writing)

Signature and Dates

I declare, under penalty of perjury under the laws of the State of Washington, the information contained in these Worksheets is complete, true, and correct.

_____   _____
Mother's Signature   Father's Signature

_____ _____   _____ _____
Date   City   Date   City

_____   _____
Judge/Reviewing Officer   Date

**This worksheet has been certified by the State of Washington Office of the Administrator for the Courts.
Photocopying of the worksheet is permitted.**

CHILD SUPPORT ORDER SUMMARY REPORT

Father's Name _____   Mother's Name _____

Cause Number _____   County _____

Date of Order _____   Summary Report Filed By: Father ( )   Mother ( )

1. Type of Order (check one):   ___ Superior Court   ___ Administrative Law Judge

2. Was the order for child support (check one):   ___ original order for support   ___ order modifying support

3. Number of children of the parties: _____

4. List each child's age below:

   Child 1 _____   Child 2 _____   Child 3 _____   Child 4 _____

Complete lines 5-13 using the amounts entered on the child support worksheets signed by the judge/reviewing officer.

5. Father's monthly net income (Support Worksheet page 1, Line 3) $_____

6. Mother's monthly net income (Support Worksheet page 1, Line 3) $_____

7. List the basic child support obligation for each child (from Worksheet page 1, Line 5, individual amounts)

   Child 1 _____   Child 2 _____   Child 3 _____   Child 4 _____

8. Health Care Expenses (Support Worksheet page 1, Line 8f) $_____

9. Day Care and Special Expenses (Support Worksheet page 2, Line 9)

   a. Day Care Expenses $_____

   b. Education Expenses $_____

   c. Long Distance Transportation Expenses $_____

   d. Other_____ $_____

   e. Other_____ $_____

10. a. Father's standard calculation support obligation (Support Worksheet page 2, Line 13) $_____

    b. Mother's standard calculation support obligation (Support Worksheet page 2, Line 13) $_____

Actual Transfer Payment Ordered and Deviation (If any)

11. Which Parent is Payor?   Father ( )   Mother ( )

12. Transfer Payment Amount Ordered By Court $_____

13. a. If the Court deviated (amount from Line 12 differs from amount on Line 10 for the payor), was the

    deviation due to: Child Needs ( ) Parental Factors ( )

    b. If the Court deviated, what were the reasons stated by the Court for the deviation?

_____

_____

14. a. Was post-secondary education provided for?   Yes ( )   No ( )

    b. If provided for, was a dollar amount ordered?   Yes ( )   No ( )

    c. If a dollar amount was ordered, enter Payor's amount $_____

Answer remaining questions only if this was an order modifying support.

15. Total amount of the support transfer payment on the previous order? $_____

16. Which parent paid the transfer payment in the previous order?   Father ( )   Mother ( )

17. Was the change in the support transfer payment, if any, phased in? Yes ( )   No ( )

18. The change in the support order was due to: (check all applicable categories) Change in residential schedules ( )

    Change in parent income ( )   Age of children ( )   Change in support schedule ( )   Other ( )

WSCSS/Summary Report 09-01-91

WASHINGTON STATE CHILD SUPPORT SCHEDULE
STANDARDS FOR THE DETERMINATION OF CHILD SUPPORT AND USE OF THE SCHEDULE

DEFINITIONS AND STANDARDS

DEFINITIONS

Unless the court clearly requires otherwise, these definitions apply to the standards following this section.

Basic child support obligation: means the monthly child support obligation determined from the economic table based on the parties' combined monthly net income and the number of children for whom support is owed.

Child support schedule: means the standards, economic table, worksheets and instructions, as defined in chapter 26.19 RCW.

Court: means a superior court judge, court commissioner and presiding and reviewing officers who administratively determine or enforce child support orders.

Deviation: means a child support amount that differs from the standard calculation.

Economic table: means the child support table for the basic support obligation provided in RCW 26.19.020.

Instructions: means the instructions developed by the Office of the Administrator for the Courts pursuant to RCW 26.19.050 for use in compiling the worksheets.

Standards: means the standards for determination of child support as provided in chapter 26.19 RCW.

Standard calculation: means the presumptive amount of child support owed as determined from the child support schedule before the court considers any reasons for deviation.

Support transfer payment: means the amount of money the court orders one parent to pay to another parent or custodian for child support after determination of the standard calculation and deviations. If certain credits and expenses are expected to fluctuate and the order states a formula or percentage to determine the additional amount or credit on an ongoing basis, the term "support transfer payment" does not mean the additional amount or credit.

Worksheets: means the forms developed by the Office of the Administrator for the Courts pursuant to RCW 26.19.050 for use in determining the amount of child support.

APPLICATION STANDARDS

1. Application of the support schedule: The child support schedule shall be applied:

    a. in each county of the state;

    b. in judicial and administrative proceedings under titles 13, 26 and 74 RCW;

    c. in all proceedings in which child support is determined or modified;

    d. in setting temporary and permanent support;

    e. in automatic modification provisions or decrees entered pursuant to RCW 26.09.100; and

    f. in addition to proceedings in which child support is determined for minors, to adult children who are dependent on their parents and for whom support is ordered pursuant to RCW 26.09.100.

The provisions of RCW 26.19 for determining child support and reasons for deviation from the standard calculation shall be applied in the same manner by the court, presiding officers and reviewing officers.

2. Written findings of fact supported by the evidence: An order for child support shall be supported by written findings of fact upon which the support determination is based and shall include reasons for any deviation from the standard calculation and reasons for denial of a party's request for deviation from the standard calculation.

3. Completion of worksheets: Worksheets in the form developed by the Office of the Administrator for the Courts shall be completed under penalty of perjury and filed in every proceeding in which child support is determined. The court shall not accept incomplete worksheets developed by the Office of the Administrator for the Courts.

4. Court review of the worksheets and order: The court shall review the worksheets and order setting child support for the adequacy of the reasons set forth for any deviation or denial of any request for deviation and for the adequacy of the amount of support ordered. Each order shall state the amount of child support calculated using the standard calculation and the amount of child support actually ordered. Worksheets shall be attached to the decree or order or if filed separately shall be initialed or signed by the judge and filed with the order.

INCOME STANDARDS

1. Consideration of all income: All income and resources of each parent's household shall be disclosed and considered by the court when the court determines the child support obligation of each parent. Only the income of the parents of the children whose support is at issue shall be calculated for the purposes of calculating the basic support obligation. Income and resources of any other person shall not be included in calculating the basic support obligation.

2. Verification of income: Tax returns for the preceding two years and current paystubs shall be provided to verify income and deductions. Other sufficient verification shall be required for income and deductions which do not appear on tax returns or paystubs.

3. Income sources included in gross monthly income: Monthly gross income shall include income from any source including: salaries; wages; contract-related benefits; income from second jobs; dividends; interest; trust income; severance pay; annuities; capital gains; pension retirement benefits; workers' compensation; unemployment benefits; spousal maintenance actually received; bonuses; social security benefits and disability insurance benefits.

Veterans' disability pensions: Veterans' disability pensions or regular compensation for disability incurred in or aggravated by service in the United States armed forces paid by the veterans' administration shall be disclosed to the court. The court may consider either type of compensation as disposable income for the purposes of calculating the child support obligation.

4. Income sources excluded from gross monthly income: The following income and resources shall be disclosed but shall not be included in gross income: income from a new spouse or income of other adults in the household; child support received from other relationships; gifts and prizes; aid to families with dependent children; supplemental security income; general assistance and food stamps. Receipt of income and resources from aid to families with dependent children, supplemental security income, general assistance, and food stamps shall not be a reason to deviate from the standard calculation.

VA aid and attendant care: Aid and attendant care payments to prevent hospitalization paid by the veterans' administration solely to provide physical home care for a disabled veteran, and special compensation paid under 38 U.S.C. Sec. 314 (k) through (r) to provide either special care or special aids, or both to assist with routine daily functions shall also be disclosed. The court may not include either aid and attendant care or special medical compensation payments in gross income for purposes of calculating the child support obligation or for the purposes of deviating from the standard calculation.

Other aid and attendant care: Payments from any source, other than veteran's aid and attendance allowance or special medical compensation paid under 38 U.S.C. Sec. 314 (k) through (r) for services provided by an attendant in case of a disability when the disability necessitates the hiring of the services of an attendant shall be disclosed but shall not be included in gross income and shall not be a reason to deviate from the standard calculation.

5. Determination of net income: The following expenses shall be disclosed and deducted from gross monthly income to calculate net monthly income: federal and state income taxes (see the following paragraph); federal insurance contributions act deductions (FICA); mandatory pension plan payments; mandatory union or professional dues; state industrial insurance premiums; court ordered spousal maintenance to the extent actually paid; up to two thousand dollars per year in voluntary pension payments actually made if the contributions were made for the two years preceding the earlier of the tax year in which the parties separated with intent to live separate and apart for the tax year in which the parties filed for dissolution; and normal business expenses and self employment taxes for self-employed persons. Justification shall be required for any business expense deduction about which there is a disagreement. Items deducted from gross income shall not be a reason to deviate from the standard calculation.

Allocation of tax exemptions: The parties may agree which parent is entitled to claim the child or children as dependents for federal tax exemptions. The court may award the exemption or exemptions and order a party to sign the federal income tax dependency exemption waiver. The court may divide the exemptions between the parties, alternate the exemptions between the parties or both.

6. Imputation of income: The court shall impute income to a parent when a parent is voluntarily unemployed or voluntarily underemployed. The court shall determine whether the parent is voluntarily underemployed or voluntarily unemployed based upon the parent's work history, education, health and age or any other relevant factors. A court shall not impute income to a parent who is gainfully employed on a full-time basis, unless the court finds that the parent is voluntarily underemployed and finds that the parent is purposely underemployed to reduce the parent's child support obligation. Income shall not be imputed for an unemployable parent. In the absence of information to the contrary, a parent's imputed income shall be based on the median income of year-round full-time workers as derived from the United States bureau of census, current populations reports, or such replacement report as published by the bureau of census. (See "Approximate Median Net Monthly Income" chart on page 27.)

ALLOCATION STANDARDS

1. Basic child support: The basic child support obligation derived from the economic table shall be allocated between the parents based on each parent's share of the combined monthly net income.

2. Health care expenses: Ordinary health care expenses are included in the economic table. Monthly health care expenses that exceed five percent of the basic support obligation shall be considered extraordinary health care expenses. Extraordinary health care expenses shall be shared by the parents in the same proportion as the basic child support obligation.

3. Day care and special child rearing expenses: Day care and special child rearing expenses, such as tuition and long distance transportation costs to and from the parents for visitation purposes, are not included in the economic table. These expenses shall be shared by the parents in the same proportion as the basic child support obligation.

4. The court may exercise its discretion to determine the necessity for and the reasonableness of all amounts ordered in excess of the basic child support obligation.

LIMITATIONS STANDARDS

1. Limit at forty-five percent of a parent's net income: Neither parent's total child support obligation may exceed forty-five percent of net income except for good cause shown. Good cause includes but is not limited to possession of substantial wealth, children with day care expenses, special medical need, educational need, psychological need and larger families.

2. Income below six hundred dollars: When combined monthly net income is less than six hundred dollars, a support order of not less than twenty-five dollars per child per month shall be entered for each parent.

Basic subsistence limitation: A parent's support obligation shall not reduce his or her net income below the need standard for one person established pursuant to RCW 74.04.770, except for the mandatory minimum payment of twenty-five dollars per child per month as required under RCW 26.19 or in cases where the court finds reasons for deviation under RCW 26.19. This section shall not be construed to require monthly substantiation of income.

3. Income above five thousand and seven thousand dollars: The economic table is presumptive for combined monthly net incomes up to and including five thousand dollars. When combined monthly net income exceeds five thousand dollars, support shall not be set at an amount lower than the presumptive amount of support set for combined monthly net incomes of five thousand dollars unless the court finds a reason to deviate below that amount. The economic table is advisory but not presumptive for monthly net income that exceeds five thousand dollars. When combined monthly net income exceeds seven thousand dollars, the court may set support at an advisory amount of support set for combined monthly net incomes between five thousand and seven thousand dollars or the court may exceed the advisory amount of support set for combined monthly net income of seven thousand dollars upon written findings of fact.

DEVIATION STANDARDS

1. Reasons for deviation from the standard calculation include but are not limited to the following:

a. Sources of income and tax planning: The court may deviate from the standard calculation after consideration of the following:

i. Income of a new spouse if the parent who is married to the new spouse is asking for a deviation based on any other reason. Income of a new spouse is not, by itself, a sufficient reason for deviation;

ii. Income of other adults in the household if the parent who is living with the other adult is asking for a deviation based on any other reason. Income of other adults in the household is not, by itself, a sufficient reason for deviation;

iii. Child support actually received from other relationships;

iv. Gifts;

v. Prizes;

vi. Possession of wealth, including but not limited to savings, investments, real estate holdings and business interests, vehicles, boats, pensions, bank accounts, insurance plans, or other assets;

vii. Extraordinary income of a child; or

viii. Tax planning considerations. A deviation for tax planning may be granted only if the child would not receive a lesser economic benefit due to the tax planning.

b. Non-recurring income: The court may deviate from the standard calculation based on a finding that a particular source of income included in the calculation of the basic support obligation is not a recurring source of income. Depending on the circumstances, non-recurring income may include overtime, contract-related benefits, bonuses or income from second jobs. Deviations for non-recurring income shall be based on a review of the non-recurring income received in the previous two calendar years.

c. Debt and high expenses: The court may deviate from the standard calculation after consideration of the following expenses:

i. Extraordinary debt not voluntarily incurred;

ii. A significant disparity in the living costs of the parents due to conditions beyond their control;

iii. Special needs of disabled children; or

iv. Special medical, educational, or psychological needs of the children.

d. Residential schedule: The court may deviate from the standard calculation if the child spends a significant amount of time with the parent who is obligated to make a support transfer payment. The court may not deviate on that basis if the deviation will result in insufficient funds in the household receiving the support to meet the basic needs of the child or if the child is receiving aid to families with dependent children (AFDC). When determining the amount of the deviation, the court shall consider evidence concerning the increased expenses to a parent making support transfer payments resulting from the significant amount of time spent with that parent and shall consider the decreased expenses, if any, to the party receiving the support resulting from the significant amount of time the child spends with the parent making the support transfer payment.

e. Children from other relationships: The court may deviate from the standard calculation when either or both of the parents before the court have children from other relationships to whom the parent owes a duty of support.

i. The child support schedule shall be applied to the mother, father and children of the family before the court to determine the presumptive amount of support.

ii. Children from other relationships shall not be counted in the number of children for purposes of determining the basic support obligation and the standard calculation.

iii. When considering a deviation from the standard calculation for children from other relationships, the court may consider only other children to whom the parent owes a duty of support. The court may consider court-ordered payments of child support for children from other relationships only to the extent that the support is actually paid.

iv. When the court has determined that either or both parents have different children from other relationships, deviations under this section shall be based on consideration of the total circumstances of both households. All child support obligations paid, received and owed for all children shall be disclosed and considered.

2. All income and resources of the parties before the court, new spouses, and other adults in the household shall be disclosed and considered as provided. The presumptive amount of support shall be determined according to the child support schedule. Unless specific reasons for deviation are set forth in the written findings of fact and are supported by the evidence, the court shall order each parent to pay the amount of support determined by using the standard calculation.

3. The court shall enter findings that specify reasons for any deviation or any denial of a party's request for any deviation from the standard calculation made by the court. The court shall not consider reasons for deviation until the court determines the standard calculation for each parent.

4. When reasons exist for deviation, the court shall exercise discretion in considering the extent to which the factors would affect the support obligation.

5. Agreement of the parties is not by itself adequate reason for any deviations from the standard calculations.

POSTSECONDARY EDUCATION STANDARDS

1. The child support schedule shall be advisory and not mandatory for postsecondary educational support.

2. When considering whether to order support for postsecondary educational expenses, the court shall determine whether the child is in fact dependent and is relying upon the parents for the reasonable necessities of life. The court shall exercise its discretion when determining whether and for how long postsecondary educational support based upon the consideration of factors that include but are not limited to the following: age of the child; the child's needs; the expectations of the parties for their children when the parties were together; the child's prospects, desires, aptitudes, abilities or disabilities; the nature of the postsecondary education sought and the parent's level of education, standard of living and current and future resources.

Also to be considered are the amount and type of support that the child would have been afforded if the parents had stayed together.

3. The child must enroll in an accredited academic or vocational school, must be actively pursuing a course of study commensurate with the child's vocational goals and must be in good academic standing as defined by the institution. The court-ordered postsecondary educational support shall be automatically suspended during the period or periods the child fails to comply with these conditions.

4. The child shall also make available all academic records and grades to both parents as a condition of receiving postsecondary educational support. Each parent shall have full and equal access to the postsecondary education records as provided by statute (RCW 26.09.225).

5. The court shall direct that either or both parents' payments for postsecondary educational expenses be made directly to the educational institution if feasible, then the court in its discretion may order that either or both parents' payments be made directly to the child if the child does not reside with either parent. If the child resides with one of the parents the court may direct that the parent making the support transfer payments make the payments to the child or to the parent who has been receiving the support transfer payments.

WASHINGTON CHILD SUPPORT SCHEDULE
WORKSHEET INSTRUCTIONS

WASHINGTON STATE CHILD SUPPORT SCHEDULE
INSTRUCTIONS FOR WORKSHEETS

Fill in the names and ages of only those child(ren) whose support is at issue.

PART I: BASIC CHILD SUPPORT OBLIGATION

Pursuant to Income Standard #1: Consideration of all income, "only the income of the parents of the children whose support is at issue shall be calculated for purposes of calculating the basic support obligation." (See page 22.)

Pursuant to Income Standard #2: Verification of income, "tax returns for the preceding two years and current paystubs are required for income verification purposes. Other sufficient verification shall be required for income and deductions which do not appear on tax returns or paystubs." (See page 22.)

GROSS MONTHLY INCOME

Gross monthly income is defined under Income Standard #3: Income sources excluded from gross monthly income. (See page 22.)

Income exclusions are defined under Income Standard #4: Income sources excluded from gross monthly income. (See page 22.) Excluded income must be disclosed and listed in Part VI of the worksheets.

Monthly Average of Income:

- If income varies during the year, divide the annual total of the income by 12.
- If paid weekly, multiply the weekly income by 52 and divide by 12.
- If paid every other week, multiply the two-week income by 26 and divide by 12.
- If paid twice a month (bi-monthly), multiply the bi-monthly income by 24 and divide by 12.

If a parent is unemployed, underemployed or the income of a parent is unknown, refer to "Income Standard #6: Imputation of income."

In the absence of information to the contrary, a parent's imputed income shall be based on the following table.

Approximate Median
Net Monthly Income

MALE	age	FEMALE
$1026	15-24	$ 916
$1631	25-34	$1257
$2042	35-44	$1396
$2086	45-54	$1381
$2031	55-65	$1249

Source: United States Bureau of Census, Current Population Reports, 1987

[Net income has been determined by subtracting FICA (7.65 percent) and the tax liability for a single person (one withholding allowance).]

Line 1a, Wages & Salaries: Enter the average monthly total of all salaries, wages, contract related benefits, income from second jobs and bonuses.

Line 1b, Interest and Dividend Income: Enter the average monthly total of dividends and interest income.

Line 1c, Business Income: Enter the average monthly income from self-employment.

WASHINGTON CHILD SUPPORT SCHEDULE
WORKSHEET INSTRUCTIONS — Continued

Line 1d, Spousal Maintenance Received: Enter the monthly amount of spousal maintenance actually received.

Line 1e, Other Income: Enter the average monthly total of other income. *(Other income includes, but is not limited to, severance pay, annuities, capital gains, pension retirement benefits, workers compensation, unemployment benefits, social security benefits, and disability insurance benefits.)*

Line 1f, Total Gross Monthly Income: Add the monthly income amounts for each parent (lines 1a through 1e) and enter the totals on line 1f.

MONTHLY DEDUCTIONS FROM GROSS INCOME

Allowable monthly deductions from gross income are defined under Income Standard #5: Determination of net income. (See page 23.)

Monthly Average of Deductions: If a deduction is annual or varies during the year, divide the annual total of the deduction by 12 to determine a monthly amount.

Line 2a, Income Taxes: Enter the monthly amount actually owed for state and federal income taxes. *(The amount of income tax withheld on a paycheck may not be the actual amount of income tax owed due to a tax refund, etc. It is appropriate to consider tax returns from prior years as indicating the actual amount of income tax owed if income has not changed.)*

Line 2b, FICA/Self-Employment Taxes:
Enter the total monthly amount of FICA/Self-Employment taxes owed.

Line 2c, State Industrial Insurance Deductions: Enter the monthly amount of state industrial insurance deductions.

Line 2d, Mandatory Union/Professional Dues: Enter the monthly cost of mandatory union or professional dues.

Line 2e, Pension Plan Payments: Enter the monthly cost of mandatory pension plan payments. *(For information regarding limitations on the allowable deduction of voluntary pension plan payments refer to Income Standard #5: Determination of income. See page 22.)*

Line 2f, Spousal Maintenance Paid: Enter the monthly amount of spousal maintenance actually paid pursuant to a court order.

Line 2g, Normal Business Expenses: If self-employed, enter the amount of normal business expenses. *(Pursuant to Income Standard #5: Determination of net income: "justification shall be required for any business expense deduction about which there is a disagreement." See page 23.)*

Line 2h, Total Deductions From Gross Income: Add the monthly deductions for each parent (lines 2a through 2g) and enter the totals on line 2h.

Line 3, Monthly Net Income: For each parent subtract total deductions (line 2h) from total gross monthly income (line 1f) and enter these amounts on line 3.

Line 4, Combined Monthly Net Income: Add the parents' monthly net incomes (line 3) and enter the total on line 4.

Line 5, Basic Child Support Obligation: In the work area provided on line 5 enter the basic support obligation amounts determined for each child. Add these amounts together and enter the total in the box on line 5. *(To determine a per child basic support obligation see the following economic table instructions.)*

Economic Table instructions

The Economic Table is located on page 14.

To use the Economic Table to determine an individual support amount for each child:

WASHINGTON CHILD SUPPORT SCHEDULE
WORKSHEET INSTRUCTIONS — Continued

- locate in the left-hand column the monthly net income amount closest to the amount entered on line 4 of Worksheet A; *(round up when the combined monthly net income falls halfway between the two amounts in the left-hand column.)*
- locate on the top row the family size for the number of children for whom child support is being determined; *(When determining family size for the required worksheets do not include children from other relationships.)*
- circle the two numbers in the columns listed below the family size that are across from the net income amount. The amount in the "A" column is the basic support amount for a child up to age 12. The amount in the "B" column is the basic support amount for a child 12 years of age or older.

Line 6, Proportional Share of Income: Divide the monthly net income for each parent (line 3) by the combined monthly net income (line 4) and enter these amounts on line 6. *(The entries on line 6 when added together should equal 1.00.)*

Line 7, Each Parent's Basic Child Support Obligation: Multiply the *total* child support obligation (amount in box on line 5) by the income share proportion for each parent (line 6) and enter these amounts on line 7. *(The amounts entered on line 7 added together should equal the amount entered on line 5.)*

PART II: HEALTH CARE, DAY CARE, AND SPECIAL CHILD REARING EXPENSES

Pursuant to Allocation Standard #4, "the court may exercise its discretion to determine the reasonableness of all amounts ordered in excess of the basic child support obligation." (See page 23.)

Pursuant to Allocation Standard #2: Health care expenses and #3: Day care and special child rearing expenses, extraordinary health care, day care and special child rearing expenses shall be shared by the parents in the same proportion as the basic support obligation. (See page 23.) **Note:** The court order should reflect that extraordinary health care, day care and special child rearing expenses should be apportioned by the same percentage as the child support obligation.

Monthly Average of Expenses: If a health care, day care, or special child rearing expense is annual or varies during the year, divide the annual total of the expense by 12 to determine a monthly amount.

HEALTH CARE EXPENSES

Line 8a, Monthly Health Insurance Premiums Paid for Child(ren): List the monthly amount paid by each parent for health care insurance for the child(ren) of the relationship. *(When determining an insurance premium amount do not include the portion of the premium paid by an employer or other third party and/or the portion of the premium that covers the parent or other household members.)*

Line 8b, uninsured monthly health care expenses: List the monthly amount paid by each parent for the child(ren)'s health care expenses not reimbursed by insurance.

Line 8c, Total Monthly Health Care Expenses: For each parent add the health insurance premium payments (line 8a) to the uninsured health care payments (line 8b) and enter these amounts on line 8c.

Line 8d, Combined Monthly Health Care Expenses: Add the parents' total health care payments (line 8c) and enter this amount on line 8d.

Line 8e, Maximum Ordinary Monthly Health Care: Multiply the basic support obligation (line 5) times .05.

Line 8f, Extraordinary Monthly Health Care Expenses: Subtract the maximum monthly health care deduction (line 8e) from the combined monthly health care payments (line 8d) and enter this amount on line 8f. *(If the resulting answer is "0" or a negative number, enter a "0.")*

Day care and special child rearing expenses

Line 9a, Day Care Expenses: Enter average monthly day care costs.

Line 9b, Education Expenses: Enter the average monthly costs of tuition and other related educational expenses.

Line 9c, Long Distance Transportation Expenses: Enter the average monthly costs of long distance travel incurred pursuant to the residential or visitation schedule.

Line 9d, Other Special Expenses: Identify any other special expenses and enter the average monthly cost of each.

Line 9e, Total Day Care and Special Expenses: Add the monthly expenses for each parent (lines 9a through 9d) and enter these totals on line 9e.

Line 10, Combined Monthly Total of Day Care and Special Expenses: Add the parents' total expenses (line 9e) and enter this total on line 10.

Line 11, Total Extraordinary Health Care, Day Care, and Special Expenses: Add the extraordinary health care payments (line 8f) to the combined monthly total of day care and special expenses (line 10) and enter this amount on line 11.

Line 12, Each Parent's Obligation for Extraordinary Health Care, Day Care, and Special Expenses: Multiply the total extraordinary health care, day care, and special expense amount (line 11) by the income proportion for each parent (line 6) and enter these amounts on line 12.

PART III: STANDARD CALCULATION SUPPORT OBLIGATION

Line 13, Standard Calculation Support Obligation: For each parent add the basic child support obligation (line 7) to the obligation for extraordinary health care, day care, and special expenses (line 12). Enter these amounts on line 13.

PART IV: CHILD SUPPORT CREDITS

Child support credits are provided in cases where parents make direct payments to third parties for the cost of goods and services which are included in the standard support obligation (e.g., payments to an insurance company or a day care provider).

Line 14a, Monthly Health Care Expenses Credit: Enter the total monthly health care expenses amounts from line 8c for each parent.

Line 14b, Day Care and Special Expenses Credit: Enter the total day care and special expenses amounts from line 9e for each parent.

Line 14c, Other Ordinary Expense Credit: If approval of another ordinary expense credit is being requested, in the space provided, specify the expense and enter the average monthly cost in the column of the parent to receive the credit. *(It is generally assumed that ordinary expenses are paid in accordance with the child's residence. If payment of a specific ordinary expense does not follow this assumption, the parent paying for this expense may request approval of an ordinary expense credit. This credit is discretionary with the court.)*

Line 14d, Total Support Credits: For each parent add the entries on lines 14 a through c and enter the totals on line 14d.

PART V: NET SUPPORT OBLIGATION/PRESUMPTION TRANSFER PAYMENT

Line 15, Net Support Obligation: For each parent, subtract the total support credits (line 14d) from the standard calculation support obligation line (line 13) and enter the resulting amounts on line 15.

Presumptive Transfer Payment: If the court does not deviate from the standard calculation, the transfer payment amount should equal the net support obligation amount of the parent who will be owing the transfer payment.

PART VI: ADDITIONAL FACTORS FOR CONSIDERATION

Pursuant to Income Standard #1: Consideration of all income, "all income and all resources of each parent's household shall be disclosed and considered by the court when the court determines the child support obligation of each parent." (See page 22.)

Separate calculations must be performed for each of the children.

Line 16 a – h Household Assets: Enter the estimated present value of assets of the household.

Line 17, Household Debt: describe and enter the amount of liens against assets owned by the household and/or any extraordinary debt.

OTHER HOUSEHOLD INCOME

Line 18a, Income of Current Spouse: If a parent is currently married to someone other than the parent of the child(ren) for whom support is being determined, list the name and enter the income of the present spouse.

Line 18b, Income of Other Adults in the Household: List the names and enter the incomes of other adults residing in the home.

Line 18c, Income of Children: if the amount is considered to be extraordinary, list the name and enter the income of children residing in the home.

Line 18d, Income from Child Support: List the name of the child(ren) for whom support is received and enter the amount of the support income.

Line 18e, Income From Assistance Programs: List the program and enter the amount of any income received from assistance programs. *Assistance programs include, but are not limited to: AFDC, SSI, general assistance, food stamps and aid and attendance allowances.)*

Line 18f, Other Income: Describe and enter the amount of any other income of the household. *(Include income from gifts and prizes on this line.)*

Line 19, Non-recurring Income: Describe and enter the amount of any income included in the calculation of gross income (line 1f) which is non-recurring. *Pursuant to Deviation Standard #1b: Non-recurring income, "depending on the circumstances, may include overtime, contract-related benefits, bonuses or income from second jobs." See page 24.)*

Line 20, Child Support Paid For Other Children: List the names and ages and enter the amount of child support paid for other children.

Line 21, Other children Living in Each Household: List the names and ages of children, other than those for whom support is being determined, who are living in each household.

Line 22, Other Factors For Consideration: In the space provided list any other factors that should be considered in determining the child support obligation. *(For information regarding other factors for consideration refer to Deviation Standards. See page 24.)*

Nonparental Custody Cases: When the children do not reside with either parent, the household income and resources of the children's custodian(s) should be listed on line 22.

IN THE SUPERIOR COURT OF THE STATE OF WASHINGTON
FOR KING COUNTY

In Re the Marriage of

<table>
<tr><td></td><td>)</td><td></td></tr>
<tr><td></td><td>)</td><td></td></tr>
<tr><td>JANE HOOD</td><td>)</td><td>No. D564</td></tr>
<tr><td></td><td>)</td><td>Separation and Property</td></tr>
<tr><td>WIFE</td><td>)</td><td>Settlement Agreement</td></tr>
<tr><td></td><td>)</td><td></td></tr>
<tr><td>JOHN HOOD</td><td>)</td><td></td></tr>
<tr><td></td><td>)</td><td></td></tr>
<tr><td>HUSBAND</td><td>)</td><td></td></tr>
<tr><td></td><td>)</td><td></td></tr>
</table>

THIS AGREEMENT, made and entered into this 20th day of February , 199- , by and between Jane Hood hereinafter called "wife," and John Hood hereinafter called "husband."

WITNESSETH:

The parties are husband and wife and have been so since the 23rd day of October, 1980 when married at Portland Oregon. The following is a list of all children born to this marriage: Jennifer Lee Hood, born March 25, 1983 Edward John Hood, born October 22, 1987. No additional children are presently contemplated and the wife is not pregnant at this time.

In consequence of disputes and irreconcilable differences, the parties separated on December 18 , 199- and from that day forth have been living apart. In view of their intention to continue to live apart for the foreseeable future, they desire to settle their respective property rights and agree on provisions for division of their properties and liabilitiesand for support of the minor children, along with custody and visitation of those children.

NOW, THEREFORE, in consideration of the mutual promises and agreements contained in this instrument, the parties agree as follows:

1. <u>Separation:</u> The parties shall at all times after the date of December 18, 199-, continue to live separate and apart, free from interference from each other, and each party may reside at the place or places he or she may select.

2. <u>Parenting Plan.</u>

The agreed Parenting Plan WPF DR 01.0400 is attached. (**Note:** See Sample #6 for an example of a Parenting Plan.)

3. <u>Child Support</u>

Paying parent: <u>John Hood</u>
        (name)

<u>216-1302 Townhouse Street, Seattle, Washington 92622</u>
        (address)

<u>Honest Ed's Autobody</u>
        (employer)

<u>123 Main Street, Seattle, Washington</u>
        (employer's address)

Receiving parent: <u>Jane Hood</u>
        (name)

<u>1313 Blueview Terrace, Edmonds, Washington 98020</u>
        (address)

<u>Hinklé's Department Store</u>
        (employer)

<u>321 Avenue Road, Seattle, Washington</u>
        (employer's address)

Amount(s) per month <u>$ 701.00</u> per month per child Date(s) due <u>on the 15th day of</u> <u>each month beginning March 15, 199-</u>

Child support shall terminate on: _____

Paid to <u>Jane Hood</u>
        (Parent directly/Washington State Support Registry)

<u>Father</u> shall pay <u>60%</u> of uninsured health care for the children;
        (Mother/Father)

other parent shall pay the remainder.

The current total monthly day care expenses of the child(ren) are: $<u>100.00</u>.

<u>Mother</u> shall pay <u>40%</u> of day care; other parent shall
        (Mother/Father)

pay the remainder.

Other costs or special needs _____

Monthly income of Mother $<u>850.00</u>   Father $<u>1,900.00</u>

Social Security Nos: Mother <u>426-22-634</u> Father <u>422-38-926</u>

Names of children and Social Security Nos:

<u>Jennifer Lee Hood SSN: 673-21-261   Edward John Hood SSN: 849-62-734</u>

Both parents shall notify the Washington State Support Registry of any changes of address or employment, if child support is being paid through the Registry.

Both parents are ordered to maintain any health insurance on the minor child(ren) which is available through a present or future employer or other organization, provided that the employer or other organization pays part or all of the premium.

If a support payment as provided for is past due in an amount equal to or greater than the support payable for one month, a notice requiring mandatory payroll deduction may be issued, or other income withholding action under Chapter 26.18 RCW or Chapter RCW 74.20A may be taken, without further notice to the parent obligated to pay support.

The receiving parent may be required to submit an accounting of how the support is being spent to benefit the child(ren).

4. Income Tax Exemption: Husband shall be allowed to claim `Jennifer Lee Hood` as an exemption on his annual income tax return and for the purpose of any applicable tax credits, so long as he is making child support payments under the terms of this Agreement. Wife shall be allowed to claim `Edward John Hood` as an exemption on her annual income tax return and for the purposes of any applicable tax credits. Each parent will execute all documents necessary to carry out this provision.

5. Division of Personal Property: Husband and wife mutually agree that all of the following property will be the sole property of the husband, upon which the wife shall have no claim whatsoever from the date of this agreement:

`Furniture now located in the den of the residence which wife and the children are continuing to reside in, together with a 1984 Ford and all household goods, personal effects and other personal property now in the possession or custody or under the control of husband.`

Husband and wife mutually agree that all of the following property will be the sole property of the wife, upon which the husband shall have no claim whatsoever from the date of this agreement:

`All household goods, furniture, personal effects, and other property now located at the residence in which she is residing with the exception of the furniture in the den, together with a 1981 Dodge Colt station wagon.`

6. Division of Real Property: For valuable consideration, husband conveys and quit claims all interest that he may have in the residence of the parties commonly known as `1313 Blueview Terrace, Edmonds, Washington, 98020`, or more particularly described as:

`Lot 1, Block 2, Section3, Edmonds, Washington`

(YOU MUST GIVE LEGAL DESCRIPTION OF REAL ESTATE HERE)

Husband further assigns to wife any and all amounts in the reserve account held by the mortgagee, `Washington Federal Savings and Loan Association`, for purposes of payment of taxes and insurance on the property described above.

7. Payment of Debts and other Obligations: Husband hereby agrees to continue to pay, and hold the wife harmless from any liability thereon, the following described debts and obligations:

Creditor	Approximate Balance
Al's Auto Sales	$1,135.72
Seattle-First National Bank MasterCard	672.56
Household Finance Company	3,073.77
Sears & Roebuck	300.00
Penney's	158.73
Coast Guard Federal Credit Union at Alameda, California	4,400.00
Credit Thrift	934.90
Avco Finance Company	963.75

Wife hereby agrees to continue to pay, and hold the husband harmless from any liability thereon, the following obligations:

Creditor	Approximate Balance
Washington Federal Savings & Loan Association	$31,784.08

This obligation is secured by a Deed of Trust on the residence and real property which is conveyed to wife pursuant to the terms of Paragraph 6 above.

Union 76 Oil Company	Revolving

8. Payment of Obligations After Date of Execution of this Agreement: The parties hereto agree that all obligations incurred by husband or wife after the date of the execution of this agreement shall be his or her separation obligation, and he or she will pay in full, when due, all such obligations and shall hold the other party harmless in event of any liability resulting therefrom.

9. Insurance Policies: Husband and wife mutually agree that any and all interest and incidents of ownership of any policies of life insurance shall be awarded to the party whose life is insured and that party shall be responsible for making all premium payments thereon. Husband agrees to keep full force and effect his Serviceman's Group Life Insurance policy in the face amount of $20,000.00 and to name his children by Jane Hood named on page one above as beneficiaries so long as each is under 18 years of age or is otherwise not emancipated as that term is defined in Paragraph 3. In the event of husband's separation or retirement from active duty with the U.S. Coast Guard or if for any other reason said Serviceman's Group Life Insurance is no longer available to husband or in force the husband agrees to obtain substitute life insurance coverage in a minimum face amount of $20,000.00 and to name his children identified above as beneficiaries for a like term.

10. 199- Income Tax Refund: The parties hereto agree that any tax refund resulting from payment of 199- Federal Income Taxes shall be divided equally between husband and wife.

11. <u>Income Tax Returns:</u> It is understood and agreed that husband and wife may file a joint income tax return for any year for which the law authorizes it and which may be affected by this agreement; and each party fully agrees to cooperate in the preparation and execution of any such joint income tax returns.

12. <u>Pensions, Retirement Pay, Etc.:</u> Each of the parties has or may acquire in the future, through membership in labor unions, trade associations, fraternal organizations or other organizations of similar type or through his or her employment, life insurance, accident insurance or health insurance on his or her life, and has or may acquire investments in retirement plans, disability insurance plans, and pension or social security rights. The parties agree that any said insurance or rights shall be the sole property of the party through whose membership or employment the same has been or will be acquired.

13. <u>Representations:</u> The parties represent to each other:

A. Each has made a full disclosure to the other of his or her current financial condition;

B. Each party understands and agrees that this agreement constitutes the entire contract of the parties. It supersedes all prior understandings or agreements between the parties upon the subject matters covered in this agreement.

C. The parties agree that this Separation and Property Settlement Agreement is fair and equitable at the time of its execution.

14. <u>Dissolution of Marriage:</u> The parties hereto acknowledge that wife has filed an action in the Superior Court of King county under Cause No. D564 for the dissolution of the marriage of the parties, and each of the parties to this agreement agrees that he or she will make no prayer for any division of property, support or maintenance inconsistent with any of the terms of this agreement, and the other party shall not contest any terms of said dissolution of marriage which is consistent with this agreement.

Jane Hood
JANE HOOD

John Hood
JOHN HOOD

STATE OF WASHINGTON   )
)ss.

COUNTY OF KING   )

    On this day personally appeared before me Jane Hood to me known to be the individual described in and who executed the foregoing Separation and Property Settlement Agreement, and acknowledged that she signed the same as her free and voluntary act and deed, for the uses and purposes therein mentioned.

    GIVEN under my hand and official seal this 20th day of February , 199-.

I. M. Notary
_____
Notary Public in and for the State of
Washington, residing at Edmonds

STATE OF WASHINGTON   )
)ss.

COUNTY OF   KING   )

    On this day personally appeared before me John Hood to me known to be the individual described in and who executed the foregoing Separation and Property Settlement Agreement and acknowledged that he signed the same as his free and voluntary act and deed, for the uses and purposes therein mentioned.

GIVEN under my hand and official seal this 20th day of February , 199-.

I. M. Notary
_____
Notary Public in and for the State of
Washington, residing at Edmonds

WPF DR 04.0150 (8/91)

SUPERIOR COURT OF WASHINGTON
COUNTY OF SPOKANE

In re the Marriage of:

SUE SNOOPIE,　　　　　　　Petitioner
and
SAM SNOOPIE,　　　　　　　Respondent.

NO.　92000

MOTION/DECLARATION--EX
PARTE RESTRAINING ORDER
--ORDER TO SHOW CAUSE
(RSTOSC)

CLERK'S ACTION REQUIRED

I. MOTION

Based upon the declaration below, I move the court for a temporary restraining order without written or oral notice to my spouse or to my spouse's lawyer.

1.1　I request that the court RESTRAIN:

[x]　each party from transferring, removing, encumbering, concealing or in any way disposing of any property except in the usual course of business or for the necessities of life and requiring each party to notify the other of any extraordinary expenditures made after the order is issued.

[x]　each party from molesting or disturbing the peace of the other party or of any child.

[ ]　_____ from entering the
　　　　　　　　　　　　(Name)
residence at _____.
　　　　　　　　　　　　　(Address)

[x]　each party from entering the home of the other party.

[x]　each party from removing any of the children from the State of Washington.

[x]　each party from assigning, transferring, borrowing, lapsing, surrendering or changing entitlement of any insurance policies of either or both parties whether medical, health, life or auto insurance.

[ ]　other:

EX PARTE RESTRAINING ORDER
CR 65(b); RCW 26.09.060
Page 1

WPF DR 04.0150 (8/91)

1.2 SURRENDER OF DEADLY WEAPONS.

[x] Does not apply.
[ ] I also request that the court require my spouse to surrender any deadly weapon in his or her immediate possession or control or subject to his or her immediate possession or control to the sheriff of the county having jurisdiction of this proceeding, to his or her lawyer or to a person designated by the court. Clear and convincing reasons for this request are set forth in the declaration below.

1.3 I also request that the other party be required to appear and show cause why the restraints requested in this motion should not be continued in full force and effect pending final determination of this action.

1.4 This motion is based on the declaration which follows.

1.5 Other:

Dated: January 5, 199—

Sue Snoopie

Signature of Lawyer or Moving Party (if moving party has no lawyer)

Sue Snoopie

Print or Type Name (include Washington State Bar Number, if applicable)

II. DECLARATION

It is necessary that the court issue a temporary restraining order granting the relief requested above for the reasons set forth below.

2.1 An ex parte restraining order is being requested to prevent the following injury (define the injury):
The Respondent has assaulted me in the past and I fear physical injury.

EX PARTE RESTRAINING ORDER
CR 65(b); RCW 26.09.060
Page 2

WPF DR 04.0150 (8/91)

2.2 This injury may be irreparable because:

One cannot be adequately compensated for physical injury

2.3 A temporary restraining order should be granted without written or oral notice to my spouse or my spouse's lawyer because immediate and irreparable injury, loss, or damage will result before my spouse or my spouse's lawyer can be heard in opposition. The following efforts have been made to give my spouse or my spouse's lawyer notice:

[x] I have not attempted to give notice to my spouse or my spouse's lawyer because:
He does not have a lawyer and I fear he will injure me if he knows I am filing for dissolution of our marriage.

[ ] I have attempted to give notice to my spouse or my spouse's lawyer as follows:

Reasons supporting the claim that notice should not be required are as follows:
My husband has an explosive temper and has repeatedly threatened to assault me and has in fact assaulted me.

I declare under penalty of perjury under the laws of the State of Washington that the foregoing is true and correct.

Signed at <u>Spokane, Washington</u>, on <u>January 5, 199-</u>
          (City and State)   (Date)

Sue Snoopie
          Signature
SUE SNOOPIE
Print or Type Name and Washington
State Bar Number, if applicable

EX PARTE RESTRAINING ORDER
CR 65(b); RCW 26.09.060
Page 3

WPF DR 04.0150 (8/91)

III. ORDER

3.1   This order is being issued to prevent the following injury (define the injury):

Physical injury.

3.2   This injury may be irreparable because:

one cannot be adequately compensated for physical injury.

3.3   This order is being granted without notice because:

the Respondent may threaten or injure the Petitioner if notice is given.

3.4   It is ORDERED that:

[x]   Each party is restrained from molesting or disturbing the peace of the other party or of any child.*

[X]   Each party is restrained from entering the home of the other party.*

*VIOLATION OF THE ABOVE PROVISIONS OF THIS ORDER WITH ACTUAL NOTICE OF THEIR TERMS IS A CRIMINAL OFFENSE UNDER CHAPTER 26.09 RCW, AND WILL SUBJECT THE VIOLATOR TO ARREST. RCW 26.09.060(5).

[x]   Each party is restrained from transferring, removing, encumbering, concealing or in any way disposing of any property except in the usual course of business or for the necessities of life and requiring each party to notify the other of any extraordinary expenditures made after the order is issued.

[x]   Each party is restrained from removing any of the children from the State of Washington.

[x]   Each party is restrained from assigning, transferring, borrowing, lapsing, surrendering or changing entitlement of any insurance policies of either or both parties whether medical, health, life or auto insurance.

[ ]   Other:

EX PARTE RESTRAINING ORDER
CR 65(b); RCW 26.09.060
Page 4

41

WPF DR 04.0150 (8/91)

3.5 SURRENDER OF DEADLY WEAPONS.

[X] Does not apply.
[ ] It is ordered that _____ surrender
                                    (Name)
any deadly weapon in his or her immediate possession or control or
subject to his or her immediate possession or control to:

[ ] the _____ county sheriff.
                  (Name of County)
[ ] _____.
                        (Name)

The court finds on the basis of the declaration above or the other
evidence presented that irreparable injury could result if an order is
not issued until the time for response has elapsed. (See RCW
26.09.060(2)(b).)

3.6 SHOW CAUSE ORDER.

It is ordered that __SAM SNOOPIE_____ appear and show cause,
                            (Name)
if any, why the above restraints should not be continued in full force and
effect pending final determination of this action. A hearing has been set
before _____ for the following date, time and place:
          (Judge or Commissioner)

Date:

Time: a.m./p.m.

Place:

Room/Department:

3.7 This order shall be filed forthwith in the clerk's office and entered of record.

3.8 The clerk of the court shall forward a copy of this order, on or before the
     next judicial day, to __SPOKANE COUNTY SHERIFF'S DEPT._____.
                    (Name of the appropriate law enforcement agency)

EX PARTE RESTRAINING ORDER
CR 65(b); RCW 26.09.060
Page 5

WPF DR 04.0150 (8/91)

2

3.10   <u>SPOKANE COUNTY SHERIFF'S DEPT.</u>   shall forthwith enter

4   (Name of the appropriate law enforcement agency)
this order into any computer-based criminal intelligence system available in

6   this state used by law enforcement agencies to list outstanding warrants.

8   3.11   This order shall expire on the hearing date set in paragraph 3.7 above or 14
days from the date of issuance unless otherwise extended by the court.

10

   3.12   Other:

12

14

16

18

20

22

24

26

28

30

32

34   Dated: <u> January 5, 199– </u>   *I. M. Commissioner*
          (Date and Hour of Issuance)   Judge/Commissioner

36

38   Presented by:

40   *Sue Snoopie*
     ~~Signature and Washington State Bar~~

42   ~~Number, if applicable~~
     Sue Snoopie, Petitioner
     EX PARTE RESTRAINING ORDER
     CR 65(b); RCW 26.09.060
     Page 6

3

PRELIMINARY NOTES ON PROCEDURE

a. GENERAL

The Administrator for the Courts of Washington State has developed standard *mandatory forms* for people doing their own divorce. Under Washington law, a notary is not needed for your signature on these forms. Mandatory forms have an identifying number, e.g., Form DR 04.0400, Decree of Dissolution. Blank copies of the most commonly used forms are provided at the back of this book. Use one copy for your rough work, then fill out a good copy for filing and photocopy this original to obtain the desired number of copies. Copies of mandatory forms may be obtained by contacting the clerk of the court for your county or the Office of the Administrator for the Courts at:

Office of the Administrator for the Courts
Temple of Justice, AV-01
Olympia, Washington
98504
(206) 357-2129

When there is more than one page to a form, staple the pages together in the upper left-hand corner.

b. STYLE OF CAUSE

All legal documents must have a heading known as the "style of cause" so they can be properly identified. Specifically, the style of cause in a divorce action will contain the following information.

(a) Court case number that will be stamped or written on the original and all copies of the Petition when it is filed and that should be used on all subsequent documents filed

(b) Name of the court

(c) Full names of petitioner and respondent

The style of cause will head *all* of your documents. It is preprinted on the forms. You just have to fill in the information for your case as in Sample #3.

c. FORMAT FOR COURT ORDERS THAT YOU TYPE YOURSELF

If you need to file papers that are not at the back of this book, or have no mandatory form available from the Court Administrator, follow these guidelines. For maximum clarity and legibility, courts prefer that documents be typed.

All pleadings should be on bond paper. The paper must have line numbers on its left margin. It must be 8½" x 11". Space of approximately four inches at the top of the first page of each document should be left for the clerk's stamp. All other pages should have a two-inch margin at the top and bottom.

The bottom left side of all papers should have the name of the paper, i.e., Petition, Decree or Findings of Fact, and the page number of the document printed.

Your name should be typed under your signature on each document you sign.

SAMPLE #3
STYLE OF CAUSE

IN THE SUPERIOR COURT OF THE STATE OF WASHINGTON,
COUNTY OF ANYCOUNTY

In re the Marriage of:

}	No. 007
Joan Que Public }	
PETITIONER }	**Petition for Dissolution**
}	**of Marriage**
- and - }	
}	
John Que Public }	
RESPONDENT}	

4
STEP-BY-STEP PROCEDURE

a. THE PETITION FOR DISSOLUTION OF MARRIAGE

The first step in obtaining your divorce is to fill out a Petition for Dissolution of Marriage (Form DR 01.0100; see Sample #4). This is the form that requests the Superior Court of Washington to terminate your marriage. The spouse who files the Petition is called the petitioner and the other spouse is called the respondent.

All of the forms shown in this book are required under Washington law. When you fill out the forms, be sure that each section is filled in. The forms have check boxes and you must check the correct box in each case. In some cases this will be the box that says "does not apply." Be sure to check this box if the subject matter does not apply to your case.

The Marriage Dissolution Act requires that your Petition contain the following information:

(a) The last known address of each party

(b) The date and place of marriage

(c) The date on which the parties separated

(d) The names, ages, and addresses of any children dependent upon either or both of the spouses

(e) A statement saying whether or not the wife is pregnant

(f) A parenting plan (see section 2 of Sample #1 and Sample #6)

(g) A statement as to whether there is community property to be disposed of (and how that property will be disposed of)

(h) A statement of relief sought (This statement should include a request for dissolution of the marriage and, where applicable, residential arrangements for the children; visitation desired; level of child support desired; maintenance requested; division of property; division of the debts; and a request that the property settlement attached to the Petition be approved and incorporated in the Decree of Dissolution.

Fill out your Petition carefully. Use the example in Sample #4 as a guide, but use your own information and your own words. Be sure to express yourself clearly. If a clause does not apply in your case, cross it out and fill in the particulars of your situation.

1. When you and your spouse file together

If you and your spouse have both agreed to the divorce and its terms, you may fill out the Petition together and both sign it.

When you and your spouse are cooperating like this, you should attach Form DR 01.0310, Acceptance of Service, filled out and signed by your spouse.

Now that your Petition is filled out and has been signed by you and your spouse, take the original plus two copies to the county courthouse. Pay the filing fee in cash to the cashier at the county clerk's office. The county clerk will place a number on the original and both copies and will stamp all three with the "filed" stamp showing the date you filed the papers.

The 90-day reconciliation period begins on the date stamped on your papers if your spouse has signed a Joinder of the Petition (see Sample #5). (If he or she has not signed, then the 90-day period begins only after your spouse has been served with a Petition and Summons.)

The county clerk will keep the original of your Petition and give you the stamped copies. Whenever you wish to inquire about your file from the county clerk, refer to the number on your copy. The county clerk will also ask you to fill in a vital statistics form required by the Washington State Department of Health. You will need to know your own and your spouse's place and date of birth to complete this form.

2. When you and your spouse are not filing together

If you and your spouse have both signed the Petition for Dissolution, a Summons (Form DR 01.0200) is not necessary and should not be filled out or served. But if your spouse is not cooperating, you should attach a Summons to your Petition. The Summons is a form used to notify your spouse that you have asked the court to terminate your marriage (see Sample #7).

Fill out the Summons at the same time you fill out the Petition. Then staple (in the upper left-hand corner) the Summons on top of the Petition and take both to the county clerk for filing.

Once you have filed the Summons and Petition with the county clerk, both must be served on your spouse. You cannot deliver the Summons and Petition yourself, because the law says that the papers must be served by a person who is not a party to the divorce.

There are three ways you can have the Summons and Petition served on your spouse:

(a) Take the papers to the sheriff of the county in which your spouse lives and pay the service fee.

(b) Look up the name of a process service in the Yellow Pages of your telephone book under the headings "Attorney's Service Bureaus" or "Process Servers" and call them. They will tell you how to hire their services and how much they charge.

(c) Ask a friend 18 years or older to serve it.

If your spouse lives outside the state of Washington, you must still have the Summons and Petition served. Go to the directory library of your telephone company and ask for the telephone book for the city in which your spouse lives. Look up a process server in the Yellow Pages; write to them, giving the address of your spouse and asking what the service charge will be.

Upon receiving a reply, mail the copy of the Summons and Petition, along with the required fee, to the process server in your spouse's city. (If your spouse is missing, or you cannot afford a process server, please see chapter 5, section a.) If your spouse lives in another country, you should seek legal advice to have the Summons and Petition served.

Once your spouse has been served the Summons and Petition, the sheriff or the process server will mail you a paper called a Return of Service (Form DR 01.0250). This paper proves that your spouse has been notified of the divorce proceedings (see Sample #8).

If a friend serves the papers, he or she must prepare and sign a Return of Service form. The form is available from the Office of the Administrator for the Courts.

Take the Return of Service to the county clerk's office; it will be placed in your court file. Unless this paper is in your court file (or you and your spouse have both signed the Petition), the court will not sign your

Decree of Dissolution, which grants your divorce.

If your spouse does not respond to the Petition within the time set out in the Summons, you may ask the court for an Order of Default and proceed without your spouse's consent after the 90-day reconciliation period has passed. You should do this by filing a Motion for Default and an Order of Default. (See Samples #9 and #10.)

Count the 90 days from the day he or she is served. When you ask for an Order of Default, you must present a declaration that your spouse is not a member of the armed services. (See Sample #19 and further discussion on page 77.)

b. IF YOUR SPOUSE FILES A RESPONSE

If your spouse is served with the Summons and Petition and disagrees with what you have written, he or she may file a Response within the time limit set out in the Summons. This is called contesting the divorce. Your spouse's Response must be made in Form DR 01.0300 (see Sample #14). (If you are the responding party, then you must fill out a copy of the form to respond to a petition.)

The Response is filed by your spouse in the court in which you have begun the action, and a copy is sent to you or your lawyer. The Response sets out the areas of your Petition with which your spouse disagrees. Often the Response is drawn up by a lawyer. If you receive a Response from your spouse, you have two options:

(a) Negotiate the disputed areas with your spouse. If your spouse has an attorney, try to negotiate with him or her and reach some type of agreement. This agreement would form the basis for the next steps in your divorce procedure, namely the Findings of Fact and Decree of Dissolution of Marriage. Either you or your spouse may prepare these documents based on the agreement you come to. Both these documents must be signed by both parties, either personally or through your respective attorneys.

(b) If you cannot reach an agreement, you should retain a lawyer to represent you. It is generally unwise to attempt to handle a contested case in court by yourself. It is your right, however, to do so. The procedure is this: After your spouse has filed his or her Response, go to the clerk's office and file a Notice of Trial. This notice must be filed with the clerk and served on your spouse and his or her attorney. You must make a sworn declaration that the notice has been mailed to your spouse or his or her attorney or served on one of them. This declaration must also be filed. The system of setting cases for trial varies widely from county to county, so you should ask the clerk or court administrator in charge of such settings how it is done in your county. The wait for a trial date may vary from as little as two months in some of the smaller counties to over a year in the larger ones.

c. OBTAINING TEMPORARY RESTRAINING ORDERS AND RELIEF

If you need to obtain restraining orders during the 90-day waiting period, you should file an Order to Show Cause along with the Petition for Dissolution. To obtain an Order to Show Cause, you first must make your request on a Motion and Declaration for an Order to Show Cause and Order to Show Cause (see Sample #2, Form DR 04.0150).

The Order to Show Cause (see Sample #2, item 3.6) will order the respondent to come to court on a particular date and answer whether or not he or she agrees with the things that you have asked for. To obtain the order, you must explain to the

SAMPLE #4
PETITION FOR DISSOLUTION OF MARRIAGE (DR 01.0100)

WPF DR 01.0100 (8/91)

SUPERIOR COURT OF WASHINGTON
COUNTY OF SPOKANE

In re the Marriage of:

SUE SNOOPIE,   Petitioner
and

SAM SNOOPIE,   Respondent.

NO. 92000

PETITION FOR DISSOLUTION
OF MARRIAGE
(PTDSS)

I. BASIS

1.1   This is a petition for dissolution of a marriage which is irretrievably broken.

1.2   The name and last known residence of the wife is:
Sue Snoopie, North 123 Beagle Street, Spokane, WA 99201
(first, middle, and last name;
street; city, state, zip)

1.3   The name and last known residence of the husband is:
Sam Snoopie, East 6000 - 14th Ave.,Yakima, WA 98093
(first, middle, and last name;
street; city, state, zip)

1.4   We were married on July 2,1980 at Seattle, Washington .
              (Date)   (Place)

1.5   [ ]   Husband and wife are not separated.
      [x]   Husband and wife separated on March 1, 1988 .
                                          (Date)

1.6   This court has jurisdiction over my spouse for the reasons which follow.

      [x]   My spouse is presently residing in Washington.
      [ ]   My spouse and I lived in Washington during our marriage and I
            continue to reside in this state.
      [ ]   My spouse and I lived in Washington during our marriage and I
            continue to be a member of the armed forces stationed in this state.
      [ ]   My spouse and I may have conceived a child while within Washington.
      [ ]   My spouse will be personally served in the State of Washington.
      [ ]   My spouse will consent to the jurisdiction of this court.
      [ ]   Other:

PETITION FOR DISSOLUTION OF MARRIAGE
RCW 26.09.020
Page 1

SAMPLE #4 — Continued

WPF DR 01.0100 (8/91)

2 1.7 There is community or separate property owned by the parties. The court should make an equitable division of all the property.

4

6 [ ] My recommendation for the division of the property will be filed and served at a later date.

[ ] My recommendation for the division of the property is attached.

8 [X] The property should be divided as described below.

10 [X] The wife should be awarded the parties' interest in the following property:

12   A house at North 123 Beagle Street, Spokane, Washington

14   1990 Taurus car

   Her bank accounts

16   The furniture in the family home

18   Her pension at Acme Widget Co.

20

22

24

26

  [X] The husband should be awarded the parties' interest in the following property:

28

   His pension at XYZ Corp.

30

   1985 Buick

32   His Bank account

34

36

38

40

42

PETITION FOR DISSOLUTION OF MARRIAGE
RCW 26.09.020
Page 2

WPF DR 01.0100 (8/91)

2 1.8 DEBTS AND LIABILITIES.

4 [ ] The parties have no debts and liabilities.
   [X] The parties have debts and liabilities. The court should make an
6 equitable division of all debts and liabilities.

8   [ ] My recommendation for the division of the debts and liabilities
              will be filed and served at a later date.
10   [ ] My recommendation for the division of the debts and liabilities
              is attached.
12   [X] The debts and liabilities should be divided as described below.

14   [X] The wife should be ordered to pay the following debts
                    and liabilities to the following creditors:
16
                    Nordstrom $500
18   SeaFirst MasterCard $200

20

22

24

26

28
               [X] The husband should be ordered to pay the following
30   debts and liabilities to the following creditors:

32   Visa $2,000
               Credit Union Loan $1,000
34

36

38

40

42

PETITION FOR DISSOLUTION OF MARRIAGE
RCW 26.09.020
Page 3

WPF DR 01.0100 (8/91)

1.9   SPOUSAL MAINTENANCE.

[X]   Spousal maintenance should not be ordered.
[ ]   There is a need for spousal maintenance.

       [ ]   The following arrangements for spousal maintenance have been
              made and [ ] are [ ] are not part of a written separation
              agreement:

1.10   RESTRAINING ORDER.

[X]   A restraining order should not be ordered.
[ ]   An order should be entered restraining [ ] the husband [ ] the wife
       [ ] both parties from molesting or disturbing the peace of the other
       party or of any child because:

1.11   PREGNANCY.

[X]   The wife is not pregnant.
[ ]   The wife is pregnant. The father of the unborn child is [ ] the
       husband   [ ] not the husband   [ ] unknown.

1.12   DEPENDENT CHILDREN.

[ ]   The parties have no dependent children.
[X]   There are children who are dependent upon either or both spouses.
       Support for the dependent children should be set pursuant to the
       Washington State Child Support Schedule. My Parenting Plan for
       these children:

       [X]   is attached and is incorporated by reference as part of this
              Petition.
       [ ]   will be filed and served at a later date pursuant to RCW
              26.09.181.

PETITION FOR DISSOLUTION OF MARRIAGE
RCW 26.09.020
Page 4

WPF DR 01.0100 (8/91)

2 | Paragraph 1.12 (continued)

4 | Specific Uniform Child Custody Jurisdiction Act information for each
child is set forth below. (This information must be provided
6 | separately for each child. If there is more than one dependent child,
you may attach additional copies of this page to this Petition.)

8 |

Name of child: Susie Snoopie
10 | Date of birth: 1/10/82
Mother's name: Sue Snoopie
12 | Father's name:
Sam Snoopie

14 | Present address of child: North 123 Beagle Street, Spokane, Washington

16 | (street, city, state, zip)

18 | I [ ] do [X] do not know of any person other than my spouse who
has physical custody of this child or claims to have custody or
20 | visitation rights with respect to this child.

22 | The child has lived in the following places within the last five years
(list each place, and the names and present addresses of the persons
24 | with whom the child lived during that period):

Sue and Sam Snoopie, 123 Beagle Street, Spokane, WA 99201
26 |
North 123 Beagle Street

28 |

Other Legal Proceedings Regarding this Child (RCW 26.27.090):
30 |

I [ ] have [X] have not participated as a party, witness or in any
32 | capacity, in any other litigation concerning the custody of this child
in this state or in any other state.

34 |

I [ ] do have [X] do not have information of any paternity,
36 | dependency, or custody proceeding concerning this child in a court of
this state or of any other state.

38 |

List the county, state and case number of any other legal proceedings:
40 |

42 |

PETITION FOR DISSOLUTION OF MARRIAGE
RCW 26.09.020
Page 5

WPF DR 01.0100 (8/91)

2   1.13 Other:

4   II. RELIEF REQUESTED

6   I REQUEST the Court to enter a decree of dissolution. I also REQUEST the Court to grant the relief described below.

8

   [ ]   Provide reasonable maintenance for the [ ] husband [ ] wife.
10 [X]   Approve my parenting plan for the dependent children.
   [X]   Determine support for the dependent children pursuant to the Washington
12   State Support Schedule.
   [ ]   Approve the separation agreement.
14 [X]   Dispose of property and liabilities.
   [x]   Change name of wife to: __Sue Smith_____.
16 [ ]   Change name of husband to: _____.
   [X]   Enter a permanent restraining order.
18 [ ]   Order payment of day care expenses for the children.
   [X]   Award the tax exemptions for the dependent children as follows:
20

      to the wife.

22

24 [X]   Order payment of attorney's fees, other professional fees and costs.
   [ ]   Other:

26 Dated: __January 10, 199-_____   *Sue Snoopie*
28   **Signature of Lawyer or Petitioner (if petitioner has no lawyer)**
30   Sue Snoopie
                            Print or Type Name (include Washington
32   **State Bar Number, if applicable)**

34 I declare under penalty of perjury under the laws of the State of Washington that the foregoing is true and correct.

36

  Signed at __Spokane, Washington_____, on __1/10/9-___.
38   **(City and State)**   **(Date)**
             Sue Snoopie
40   **Signature**
            Sue Snoopie
42   **Print or Type Name**

PETITION FOR DISSOLUTION OF MARRIAGE
RCW 26.09.020
Page 6

WPF DR 01.0310 (7/91)

SUPERIOR COURT OF WASHINGTON
COUNTY OF SPOKANE

In re the Marriage of:

SUE SNOOPIE,   Petitioner

and

SAM SNOOPIE,   Respondent.

NO. 92000

[x] ACCEPTANCE OF SERVICE
     (ACSR)
[x] NOTICE OF APPEARANCE
     (NTAPR)
[x] JOINDER
     (JN)

I STATE that:

1.   I am the respondent.

2.   ACCEPTANCE OF SERVICE.

      [ ]   Does not apply.
      [x]   I accept service of:

             [x]   the summons and petition in this action.
             [ ]   a parenting plan.
             [ ]   other:

3.   NOTICE OF APPEARANCE.

      [ ]   Does not apply.
      [x]   I enter my appearance, and demand notice of all further proceedings.
             I will inform the clerk of the court of any change in my address. Any
             notices may be sent to me at:
             East 6000 - 14th Ave., Yakima, WA 98093
             (street;
             city, state, zip)

ACCEPTANCE/APPEARANCE/JOINDER
RCW 26.09.030(1)
Page 1

WPF DR 01.0310 (7/91)

2 4. JOINDER.

4 [ ] Does not apply.

[x] I join in the petition. I understand that by joining in the petition, I
6 agree with the relief requested in the petition and waive any
objections I might have to the allegations of the petition.

8

I declare under penalty of perjury under the laws of the State of Washington that
10 the foregoing is true and correct.

12 Signed at ___Spokane, Washington_____, on __1/10/9–___.
(City and State)   (Date)

14 *Sam Snoopie*
Signature
16 Sam Snoopie, Respondent
Print or Type Name

18

20

22

24

26

28

30

32

34

36

38

40

42

ACCEPTANCE/APPEARANCE/JOINDER
RCW 26.09.030(1)
Page 2

SAMPLE #6
PARENTING PLAN (DR 01.0400)

WPF DR 01.0400 (7/91)

SUPERIOR COURT OF WASHINGTON
COUNTY OF SPOKANE

In re the Marriage of:

SUE SNOOPIE,   Petitioner
and

SAM SNOOPIE,   Respondent.

NO. 92000

PARENTING PLAN
[ ] PROPOSED (PP)
[ ] TEMPORARY (PPT)
[x] FINAL ORDER (PP)

I. GENERAL INFORMATION

1.1   This parenting plan is:

[X]   the final parenting plan ordered by the court.
[ ]   a temporary parenting plan.
[ ]   proposed by _____.
                              (Name)

1.2   This parenting plan applies to the following children:

Name	Birthdate
Susie Snoopie	1 / 10 /82
	/ /
	/ /
	/ /

II. BASIS FOR RESTRICTIONS

2.1   PARENTAL CONDUCT (RCW 26.09.191(1), (2)).

[X]   Does not apply.
[ ]   The [ ] father [ ] mother has engaged in the conduct which follows.

[ ]   Willful abandonment that continues for an extended period of time or substantial refusal to perform parenting functions.
[ ]   Physical, sexual or a pattern of emotional abuse of a child.
[ ]   A history of acts of domestic violence as defined in RCW 26.50.010(1) or an assault or sexual assault which causes grievous bodily harm or the fear of such harm.

PARENTING PLAN
RCW 26.09.181; 187; 194
Page 1

WPF DR 01.0400 (7/91)

2   2.2   OTHER FACTORS (RCW 26.09.191(3)).

4   [X]   Does not apply.
        [ ]   The [ ] mother's [ ] father's involvement or conduct may have an
6   adverse effect on the child's best interests because of the existence of
              the factors which follow.
8
              [ ]   Neglect or substantial nonperformance of parenting functions.
10   [ ]   A long-term emotional or physical impairment which interferes
                    with the performance of parenting functions as defined in RCW
12   26.09.004.
              [ ]   A long-term impairment resulting from drug, alcohol, or other
14   substance abuse that interferes with the performance of
                    parenting functions.
16   [ ]   The absence or substantial impairment of emotional ties
                    between the parent and child.
18   [ ]   The abusive use of conflict by the parent which creates the
                    danger of serious damage to the child's psychological
20   development.
              [ ]   A parent has withheld from the other parent access to the
22   child for a protracted period without good cause.
              [ ]   Other:
24

26

28

30   These factors [ ] serve [ ] do not serve as a current basis for
              restrictions.
32
                        III. RESIDENTIAL SCHEDULE
34
    These provisions set forth where the child(ren) shall reside each day of the year
36 and what contact the child(ren) shall have with each parent.

38 3.1   SCHEDULE FOR HOLIDAYS.

40   The residential schedule for the child(ren) for the holidays listed below is as
        follows:
42

PARENTING PLAN
RCW 26.09.181; 187; 194
Page 2

WPF DR 01.0400 (7/91)

Paragraph 3.1 (continued)	With Mother (Specify Whether Odd/Even/Every)	With Father (Specify Whether Odd/Even/Every)
New Year's Day	Even	Odd
Martin Luther King Day	Odd	Even
Presidents Day	Even	Odd
Memorial Day	Odd	Even
July 4th	Even	Odd
Labor Day	Odd	Even
Veterans Day	Even	Odd
Thanksgiving Day	Odd	Even
Christmas Eve	Even	Odd
Christmas Day	Odd	Even

[X]   For purposes of this parenting plan, a holiday shall begin and end as follows (set forth times): 10:00 a.m. to 8:00 p.m.

[ ]   Holidays which fall on a Friday or a Monday shall include Saturday and Sunday.

3.2   PRE-SCHOOL SCHEDULE.

[X]   There are no children of preschool age.
[ ]   Prior to enrollment in school, the child(ren) shall reside with the [ ] mother [ ] father, except for the following days and times when the child(ren) will reside with or be with the other parent:

From _____ to _____
          (Day and Time)   (Day and Time)
From _____ to _____
          (Day and Time)   (Day and Time)
From _____ to _____
          (Day and Time)   (Day and Time)

[ ]   Detailed description of the pre-school schedule:

PARENTING PLAN
RCW 26.09.181; 187; 194
Page 3

WPF DR 01.0400 (7/91)

3.3   SCHOOL SCHEDULE.

Upon enrollment in school, the child(ren) shall reside with the [X] mother [ ] father, except for the following days and times when the child(ren) will reside with or be with the other parent:

From _____ to _____
            (Day and Time)   (Day and Time)
From _____ to _____
            (Day and Time)   (Day and Time)
From _____ to _____
            (Day and Time)   (Day and Time)

[X]   Detailed description of the school schedule:
Father will have one weekend each month from Friday at 4:00 p.m. to
Monday morning at 8:00 a.m.

[ ]   For purposes of this parenting plan, the school year shall begin and end as follows (set forth times):

3.4   SCHEDULE FOR WINTER VACATION.

The child(ren) shall reside with the [ ] mother   [ ] father during winter vacation, except for the following days and times when the child(ren) will reside with or be with the other parent:

From _____ to _____
            (Day and Time)   (Day and Time)
From _____ to _____
            (Day and Time)   (Day and Time)

[X]   Detailed description of the schedule for winter vacation:
The parties will divide the winter scool vacation with one parent
having the child from the time school lets out until 9:00 a.m.
Christmas Day, and the other parent having the balance of the Christmas
school vacation. This will be alternated from year to year.

PARENTING PLAN
RCW 26.09.181; 187; 194
Page 4

WPF DR 01.0400 (7/91)

2   3.5   SCHEDULE FOR SPRING VACATION.

4   The child(ren) shall reside with the [ ] mother [ ] father during spring vacation, except for the following days and times when the child(ren) will
6   reside with or be with the other parent:

8   From _____ to _____
                  (Day and Time)   (Day and Time)
10   From _____ to _____
                  (Day and Time)   (Day and Time)
12

       [X]   Detailed description of the schedule for spring vacation:
14   Spring vacation will be alternated between the parties annually.

16

18   3.6   SUMMER SCHEDULE.

20   Upon completion of the school year, the child(ren) shall reside with the
       [ ] mother [ ] father, except for the following days and times when the
22   child(ren) will reside with or be with the other parent:

24   From _____ to _____
                  (Day and Time)   (Day and Time)
26   From _____ to _____
                  (Day and Time)   (Day and Time)
28   From _____ to _____
                  (Day and Time)   (Day and Time)
30

       [X]   Detailed description of the schedule for the summer:
32   The summer schedule shall be the same as the winter schedule.

34

36

38

40

42

PARENTING PLAN
RCW 26.09.181; 187; 194
Page 5

WPF DR 01.0400 (7/91)

2   3.7   VACATION WITH PARENTS.

4   [ ]   Does not apply.

       [X]   The schedule for vacation with parents is as follows:

6   Each parent shall have two uninterrupted weeks of vacation with the minor

8   child during each summer. The father shall give the mother sixty (60) days notice of the two weeks he chooses.

10   3.8   SCHEDULE FOR SPECIAL OCCASIONS.

12   The residential schedule for the child(ren) for the following special occasions (i.e., birthdays) is as follows :

	With Mother (Specify Whether Odd/Even/Every)	With Father (Specify Whether Odd/Even/Every)
Mother's Day	Every	
Father's Day		Every
Mother's Birthday	Every	
Father's Birthday		Every
_____	_____	_____
_____	_____	_____
_____	_____	_____
_____	_____	_____
_____	_____	_____
_____	_____	_____

30   3.9   PRIORITIES UNDER THE RESIDENTIAL SCHEDULE.

32   [X]   Does not apply.

       [ ]   For purposes of this parenting plan the following days shall have

34   priority:

36   [ ]   Parent's vacation over holidays, other special occasions and the residential schedule for school vacations. Holidays over

38   other special occasions and the residential schedule for school vacations. Special occasions over the residential schedule for

40   school vacations.

       [ ]   Other:

42

PARENTING PLAN
RCW 26.09.181; 187; 194
Page 6

WPF DR 01.0400 (7/91)

2   3.10   RESTRICTIONS.

4   [X]   Does not apply.
     [ ]   The following restrictions shall apply when the child(ren) spend(s)
6   time with the [ ] mother [ ] father (see paragraph 2.1):

8

10

12

     3.11   TRANSPORTATION ARRANGEMENTS.
14
     Transportation arrangements for the child(ren), other than costs, between
16   parents shall be as follows:
                    Equally shared
18

20

22

24   3.12   DESIGNATION OF CUSTODIAN.

26   The children named in this parenting plan are scheduled to reside the
     majority of the time with the [X] mother   [ ] father.   This parent is
28   designated the custodian of the child(ren) solely for purposes of all other
     state and federal statutes which require a designation or determination of
30   custody.   This designation shall not affect either parent's rights and
     responsibilities under this parenting plan.
32
     3.13   OTHER:
34

36

38

40

42

PARENTING PLAN
RCW 26.09.181; 187; 194
Page 7

WPF DR 01.0400 (7/91)

IV. DECISION MAKING

4.1 Each parent shall make decisions regarding the day-to-day care and control of each child while the child is residing with that parent, except as provided below.

4.2 Decisions regarding each child shall be made as follows:

Education decisions   [ ] mother [ ] father [x] joint
Non-emergency health care   [ ] mother [ ] father [x] joint
Religious upbringing   [X] mother [ ] father [ ] joint
Driver's License   [ ] mother [ ] father [x] joint
Entry into Military   [ ] mother [ ] father [X] joint
Marriage before 18   [ ] mother [ ] father [x] joint
_____   [ ] mother [ ] father [ ] joint

4.3 RESTRICTIONS.

[X] Does not apply.
[ ]   Sole decision making shall be ordered to the [ ] mother [ ] father for the following reasons:

[ ]   A limitation on the other parent's decision-making authority is mandated by RCW 26.09.191.
[ ]   Both parents are opposed to mutual decision making.
[ ]   One parent is opposed to mutual decision making, and such opposition is reasonably based on the following criteria:

(a)   The existence of a limitation under RCW 26.09.191;
(b)   The history of participation of each parent in decision making in each of the areas in RCW 26.09.184(4)(a);
(c)   Whether the parents have demonstrated ability and desire to cooperate with one another in decision making in each of the areas in RCW 26.09.184(4)(a); and
(d)   The parents' geographic proximity to one another, to the extent that it effects their ability to make timely mutual decisions.

PARENTING PLAN
RCW 26.09.181; 187; 194
Page 8

WPF DR 01.0400 (7/91)

2

V. DISPUTE RESOLUTION

4   [ ]   No dispute resolution process, except court action, shall be ordered, because [ ] a limiting factor under RCW 26.09.191 applies or [ ] one parent is unable
6   to afford the cost of the proposed dispute resolution process.

8   [x]   Disputes between the parties shall be submitted to (list person or agency):

10   [ ]   counseling by _____, or
     [X]   mediation by <u>ABC Mediation Services</u>_____, or
12   [ ]   arbitration by _____.

14   The cost of this process shall be allocated between the parties as follows:

16   [ ]   _____% mother _____% father.
     [X]   based on each party's proportional share of income from line 6 of the
18   child support worksheets.
     [ ]   as determined in the dispute resolution process.

20

   The counseling, mediation or arbitration process shall be commenced by
22   notifying the other party by [X] written request [ ] certified mail [ ] other:

24

26   In the dispute resolution process:

28   (a)   Preference shall be given to carrying out this Parenting Plan.
     (b)   Unless an emergency exists, the parents shall use the designated
30   process to resolve disputes relating to implementation of the plan, except those related to financial support.
32   (c)   A written record shall be prepared of any agreement reached in counseling or mediation and of each arbitration award and shall be
34   provided to each party.
     (d)   If the court finds that a parent has used or frustrated the dispute
36   resolution process without good reason, the court shall award attorneys' fees and financial sanctions to the other parent.
38   (e)   The parties have the right of review from the dispute resolution process to the superior court.

40

42

PARENTING PLAN
RCW 26.09.181; 187; 194
Page 9

WPF DR 01.0400 (7/91)

2

VI. OTHER PROVISIONS

4

[X]   There are no other provisions.
6   [ ]   There are the following other provisions:

8

10

12

14

16

18

20

22

24

26

28

30

VII. DECLARATION

32

I declare under penalty of perjury under the laws of the State of Washington that
34   this plan has been proposed in good faith and that the statements in Part II of this
Plan are true and correct.

36

Jne Snoopie   4/13/9– Spokane Washington
38   Mother   Date and Place of Signature

Sam Snoopie   4/13/9– Spokane, Washington
40   Father   Date and Place of Signature

42

PARENTING PLAN
RCW 26.09.181; 187; 194
Page 10

WPF DR 01.0400 (7/91)

2   VIII. ORDER BY THE COURT

4

WARNING: Violation of residential provisions of this order with actual knowledge
6   of its terms is punishable by contempt of court and may be a criminal offense
under RCW 9A.40.070(2). Violation of this order may subject a violator to arrest.
8

When mutual decision making is designated but cannot be achieved, the parties
10 shall make a good faith effort to resolve the issue through the dispute resolution
process.
12

If a parent fails to comply with a provision of this plan, the other parent's
14 obligations under the plan are not affected.

16 The parenting plan set forth above is adopted and approved as an order of this
court.
18

Dated: _____ 4/15/9- _____   *J. M. Commissioner*
20   Judge/Commissioner

22

Presented by: Approved for entry:
24

26 _Sue Snoopie_ _____   _____
Signature and Washington State Bar   Signature and Washington State Bar
28 Number, if applicable   Number, if applicable

30

32

34

36

38

40

42

PARENTING PLAN
RCW 26.09.181; 187; 194
Page 11

WPF DR 01.0200 (8/91)

SUPERIOR COURT OF WASHINGTON
COUNTY OF SPOKANE

In re the Marriage of:	**NO.** 92000
SUE SNOOPIE, Petitioner	**SUMMONS**
and	**(SM)**
SAM SNOOPIE, Respondent.	

TO THE RESPONDENT:

1. The petitioner has started an action in the above court requesting:

   [X]   that your marriage be dissolved.
   [ ]   a legal separation.
   [ ]   that your marriage be declared invalid.

   Additional requests, if any, are stated in the petition, a copy of which is attached to this summons.

2. You must respond to this summons and petition by serving a copy of your written response on the person signing this summons and by filing the original with the clerk of the court. If you do not serve your written response within 20 days (or 60 days if you are served outside of the State of Washington) after the date this summons was served on you, exclusive of the day of service, the court may enter an order of default against you, and at the end of 90 days after service and filing, the court may, without further notice to you, enter a decree and approve or provide for the relief requested in the petition. If you serve a notice of appearance on the undersigned person, you are entitled to notice before an order of default or a decree may be entered.

3. Your written response to the summons and petition must be on forms approved by the Office of the Administrator for the Courts. These forms may be obtained by contacting the clerk of the court, or by contacting the Office of the Administrator for the Courts at:

   Office of the Administrator for the Courts
   Temple of Justice, AV-01
   Olympia, Washington 98504
   (206) 357-2129

SUMMONS
CR 4.1
Page 1

SAMPLE #7 — Continued

WPF DR 01.0200 (8/91)

4. If this action has not been filed with the court, you may demand that the petitioner file this action with the court. If you do so, the demand must be in writing and must be served upon the person signing this summons. Within 14 days after you serve the demand, the petitioner must file this action with the court, or the service on you of this summons and petition will be void.

5. If you wish to seek the advice of an attorney in this matter, you should do so promptly so that your written response, if any, may be served on time.

6. One method of serving a copy of your response on the petitioner is to send it by certified mail with return receipt requested.

This summons is issued pursuant to Superior Court Civil Rule 4.1 of the State of Washington.

Dated: __1/10/9-__

Sue Snoopie
_____
Signature of Lawyer or Petitioner (if petitioner has no lawyer)

Sue Snoopie
_____
Print or Type Name (include Washington State Bar Number, if applicable)

FILE ORIGINAL WITH THE CLERK OF THE COURT AT:

SERVE A COPY OF YOUR RESPONSE ON:

[x] Petitioner
[ ] Petitioner's Lawyer

__SPOKANE SUPERIOR COURT__
(Name of Court)

SUE SNOOPIE
_____
(Name)

_____
(Address)

North 123 Beagle Street
_____
(Address)

_____

Spokane, WA 99201
_____

Phone: _____

SUMMONS
CR 4.1
Page 2

WPF DR 01.0250 (7/91)

SUPERIOR COURT OF WASHINGTON
COUNTY OF YAKIMA

In re the Marriage of:

NO. 92000

SUE SNOOPIE,   Petitioner

RETURN OF SERVICE
(DOMESTIC RELATIONS)

and

(RTS)

SAM SNOOPIE,   Respondent.

I DECLARE:

1.   I am a citizen of the State of Washington, I am over the age of 18 years,
        and I am not a party to this action.

2.   I served Sam Snoopie   with the following documents:
                   (Name of Person Served)

        [X] a summons, a copy of which is attached, and a petition in this action.
        [X] a parenting plan.
        [X] other: Restraining Order and Order to Show Cause; a Motion
                    for Temporary Relief

3.   The date, time and place of service were (if by mail refer to §1.4 below):

        Date: 1/10/9–   Time: 10:00 p.m.

        Address: East 6000 – 14th Ave., Yakima. WA 98093

RETURN OF SERVICE
CR 4(g); RCW 4.28.080(14)
Page 1

WPF DR 01.0250 (7/91)

2   4.   Service was made pursuant to Civil Rule 4(d)

4   [X]   by delivery to the person named in paragraph 1.2 above.

6   [ ]   by delivery to _____, a person

                                        (Name)

8   of suitable age and discretion residing at the respondent's usual abode.

10   [ ]   by mailing two copies postage prepaid to the person named in the

             order entered by the court on _____.

12   (Date)

             One copy was mailed by ordinary first class mail, the other copy was

14   sent by certified mail return receipt requested. (Attach return receipt

             below.) The copies were mailed on _____.

16   (Date)

18   [ ]   by publication as provided in RCW 4.28.100. (A copy of the

             summons is attached.)

20

22   I declare under penalty of perjury under the laws of the State of Washington that

    the foregoing is true and correct.

24

    Signed at _____Yakima, Washington_____, on _1/10/9-_.

26   (City and State)   (Date)

28   Fees: *Percy Service*

      Service   _____   Signature

30   Mileage   _____   PERCY SERVICE

      Total   _____   Typed Name

32

34   (Attach Return Receipt here, if service was by mail)

36

38

40

42

RETURN OF SERVICE
CR 4(g); RCW 4.28.080(14)
Page 2

SAMPLE #9
MOTION FOR DEFAULT (DR 03.0100)

WPF DR 03.0100 (7/91)

SUPERIOR COURT OF WASHINGTON
COUNTY OF SPOKANE

In re the Marriage of:

SUE SNOOPIE,   Petitioner

and

SAM SNOOPIE,   Respondent.

NO.   92000

MOTION FOR DEFAULT
(MTDFL)

I. MOTION

The petitioner moves the court for an order of default. Venue of this action is proper as set forth in the Declaration below.

Dated: _February 2, 199–_

Sue Snoopie

Signature of Lawyer or Moving Party (if party has no lawyer)

SUE SNOOPIE

Print or Type Name (include Washington State Bar Number, if applicable)

II. DECLARATION

2.1   The court has proper jurisdiction and venue pursuant to the allegations of the petition at the time of filing.

The petitioner resides in ____Spokane County, Washington.____
                              (County and State)

The child(ren) reside(s) in ____Spokane County, Washington.____
                              (County and State)

Respondent resides in ____Yakima County, Washington.____
                              (County and State)

[ ]   Other:

MOTION FOR DEFAULT
CR 55(a); RCW 26.09.030
Page 1

WPF DR 03.0100 (7/91)

2   2.2   This court has jurisdiction over the respondent for the reasons which follow.

4

          [X]   The respondent is presently residing in Washington.

6   [ ]   The respondent and I lived in Washington during our marriage and I continue to reside in this state.

8   [ ]   The respondent and I lived in Washington during our marriage and I continue to be a member of the armed forces stationed in this

10   state.

          [ ]   The respondent and I may have conceived a child while within

12   Washington.

          [ ]   The respondent was personally served in the State of Washington.

14   [ ]   The respondent agreed to submit to the jurisdiction of this court.

16   2.3   Respondent was served with petition on __1/10/9-__ in __Washington State__.

                                                 (Date)   (State)

18

    2.4   More than twenty days have elapsed, if served within the State of

20   Washington, or sixty days have elapsed, if served outside of the State of Washington, since the date of service.

22

    2.5   [X]   Respondent has failed to appear.

24   [ ]   Respondent has appeared, but has failed to respond.

26   2.6   Respondent is not on active duty in the U.S. armed forces.

28   2.7   Other:

30

32   I declare under penalty of perjury under the laws of the State of Washington that the foregoing is true and correct.

34

    Signed at __Spokane, Washington__, on __2/2/9-__.

36   (City and State)   (Date)

                                    Sue Snoopie

38   Signature

                               __SUE SNOOPIE__

40   Print or Type Name and Washington State Bar Number, if applicable

42

MOTION FOR DEFAULT
CR 55(a); RCW 26.09.030
Page 2

WPF DR 03.0200 (7/91)

**SUPERIOR COURT OF WASHINGTON
COUNTY OF** SPOKANE

In re the Marriage of:

SUE SNOOPIE,   Petitioner

and

SAM SNOOPIE,   Respondent.

NO. 92000

**ORDER OF DEFAULT
(ORDFL)**

I. BASIS

A motion for default against the respondent has been presented.

II. FINDINGS

The Court FINDS that:

2.1   The court has proper jurisdiction and venue.

2.2   The respondent was served with petition, summons, a proposed parenting plan, if any, and _n/a_____ on _1/10/9-___.
                                                                    (Date)

2.3   More than twenty days have elapsed, if served within the State of Washington, or sixty days have elapsed, if served outside the State of Washington, since the date of service.

2.4   [X]   The respondent has failed to appear.
       [ ]   The respondent has appeared but has failed to respond.

III. ORDER

IT IS ORDERED that the respondent is in default.

Dated: _February 2, 199-_____   _J. M. Commissioner_____
                                             Judge/Commissioner

Presented by:

_Sue Snoopie_____
Signature and Washington State Bar
Number, if applicable

ORDER OF DEFAULT
CR 55(a); RCW 26.09.030
Page 1

court, in the Declaration (Part II of this form), what you wish the court to do. Use your own words to describe what you want and why you feel the court should order that this be granted.

After you have filled out the Motion and your Declaration and signed it (if you use the declaration form, you do not need to have it notarized), go to the Superior Court and have the judge or commissioner sign the Order to Show Cause. The Motion and Order to Show Cause must then be filed with the county clerk, and a copy of each must be served on your spouse at least eight days before the Motion is to be heard. If you are unable to serve your spouse in time, redo the order by simply writing "Alias" above the words "Order to Show Cause" and having the judge sign a new Order and assign a new date. Be sure that you serve all of the papers, including the first Order to Show Cause, the alias Order to Show Cause, your Declaration, and your Motion for an Order to Show Cause. Please see section a. 2. of this chapter for the proper service methods that you must use.

In some counties, you must call the court to confirm that you are in fact proceeding with your Motion. When you file your Motion and Order to Show Cause, check with the clerk of the court to confirm where you must call to confirm, and any time limits for confirming your Motion.

On the day of the hearing, you must appear at the court to argue for the things that you have asked for or the court will simply strike your Motion and you will not get an Order. After the judge has told you what will be granted, then you must prepare the Temporary Order (see Sample #13), sign it, and if your spouse has appeared, have your spouse sign that he or she received a copy. Then ask the judge to sign the Order. If your spouse will not sign the Order, you need a Notice of Motion on which you should

write "Note of Presentation" setting a date to present the Order in the form that you have drawn it up to the judge. Serve the Notice of Motion on your spouse by mail, along with a copy of the Order that you will present. You must file an Affidavit of Mailing with the clerk, along with the Notice, and on the day that you have set the hearing, present the Order to the court. Normally the court will sign the Order you have requested, if it is consistent with what the judge feels that he or she has ordered.

d. OBTAINING TEMPORARY ORDERS OTHER THAN RESTRAINING ORDERS

If you wish to obtain temporary orders for —

(a) a Temporary Parenting Plan (a custody and visitation order),

(b) child support,

(c) an order that entitles you to the temporary use of personal property, or

(d) an order requiring your spouse to pay certain debts,

you must serve a Motion for Temporary Order, Form DR 04.0100, on your spouse (see Sample #11). In addition to the declaration in Form DR 04.0100, you must fill out the Declaration in Support of Proposed Parenting Plan, Form DR 04.0120 (see Sample #12). You will also have to sign a Note for Dissolution Calendar and have it served on your spouse (see Sample #18).

When the judge has ordered a temporary parenting plan, Form DR 01.0400 (see Sample #6) is attached to the parenting plan as a separate order. The parenting plan should be filled out and in this case, the box at the top marked "temporary" should be checked.

The Order of Child Support, Form DR 01.0500, (see Sample #17), is always a separate order from the remaining orders. The remaining temporary orders are found in Form DR 04.0250 (see Sample #13).

e. SETTING A COURT DATE AND PREPARING FOR COURT

If your spouse does not respond to your Summons and Petition, your divorce is non-contested, and is called a default divorce. You must wait 90 days from filing and service of your Petition before you can appear in court and be granted your Decree of Dissolution. During this 90-day period you should do the following:

(a) Go to the county clerk's office and ask to look at your file. The number stamped on your Petition will help the county clerk find your file. Check to see that all your papers are in the file: Petition, Summons, and Return of Service showing that your spouse has received your Summons. The Return of Service is not necessary if you and your spouse have filed together.

(b) Once you have checked your file, ask the county clerk if any other papers are necessary before you can set a court date. The form for setting a non-contested hearing is Form DR 03.0300, the Note for Dissolution Calendar (see Sample #18).

(c) Now you can ask the county clerk to place your case on the default divorce docket. In some counties, the court administrator and not the county clerk will place your case on the default divorce docket.

(d) Make a note of your court date. Should you miss it, the court will move on to the next case, and you will have to set another date.

Now that your court date has been set, you should prepare yourself for your appearance in court. You may want to ask the county clerk if there are any other default divorce files that you could look at. Reading these other default divorce files will give you an idea of what is expected of you. You should also sit in on some default divorces being heard in court. Ask the county clerk when such divorces are being heard, and whether it is permissible to be present.

f. PREPARING THE FINAL DOCUMENTS

1. Findings of Fact

Although the Findings of Fact and Conclusions of Law, Form DR 04.0300 (see Sample #15), and the Decree of Dissolution, Form DR 04.0400 (see Sample #16) are two separate documents, they are prepared together and contain many of the same provisions.

The Findings of Fact are just what the name implies: the court's findings on the relevant facts concerning the couple's community property, the fitness of one or both parties regarding parenting functions, the distribution of debts, the amount of child support needed, visitation privileges, and so on.

When you are drawing up your Findings of Fact, keep in mind the relief you asked for originally in your Petition. If any changes are made, the court will require your spouse's approval before signing your Findings of Fact and Decree of Dissolution. Therefore, it is a good idea to follow your Petition when filling out your Findings of Fact and your Decree of Dissolution.

In the form, each of the findings is either a plain statement of a fact, such as, "the marital community has the following debts...," or a general statement upon which an order may be based (for example, "The Petitioner is a fit and proper person to have custody of the children of the parties"). It is, in fact, the purpose of the Findings of Fact to state the premises upon which the Decree of Dissolution will be based.

The Conclusions of Law determine that the Decree may legally enter and that the provisions as to residential arrangements for the children, support, maintenance, property, and debt division you have sought are reasonable and legal.

2. The Decree of Dissolution

The Decree, as one might expect, is an order setting out the final terms of the dissolution: what the residential arrangements are for the children; how the community property and community debts shall be distributed between the parties, and, sometimes, certain less common provisions that may have been at issue between the parties, such as who gets to take the income tax deduction for the children, a provision restoring the wife's former name, etc. The Decree must be signed by the judge or court commissioner; it is final and effective at that point.

Essentially, the Decree of Dissolution restates the Findings of Fact in the form of a final court order.

3. Declaration of Non-Military Service or Waiver of Rights Under Soldiers and Sailors' Civil Relief Act and Admission of Service

The Soldiers and Sailors' Civil Relief Act was passed during World War I to protect soldiers and sailors from civil actions brought against them while they were in the military. Therefore, when you, as petitioner, appear in court, you must be able to swear that your spouse, the respondent, is not in the military service or that he or she is in the military but has signed a waiver of rights.

If your spouse is not in the military, fill out a Declaration of Non-Military Service and sign it. (See Sample #19.)

If your spouse is in the military service, have him or her sign a Waiver of Rights Under the Soldiers and Sailors' Relief Act and Admission of Service before a notary public or judge advocate. (See Sample #20.)

You must bring one or the other of these forms to court with you. If your spouse is in the military and refuses to sign the waiver, you will have to get a lawyer and follow his or her advice before you proceed with your divorce.

Note that if you are a petitioner and in the military service, the Soldiers and Sailors' Civil Relief Act in no way prevents you from bringing an action for divorce. The act merely protects military people from actions against them.

g. APPEARING IN COURT

When you appear in court on the date you have set with the county clerk, you should take a seat and wait for your name to be called. The county clerk will have your file and call your name. When your name is called, walk to the front of the courtroom and take an oath to tell the truth.

You must have with you —

(a) your Findings of Fact and Conclusions of Law, and Decree of Dissolution,

(b) your Acceptance of Service/Joinder (if you and your spouse have filed jointly but your spouse is not appearing with you),

(c) your Declaration of Non-Military Service *or* Waiver of Rights under Soldiers and Sailors' Civil Relief Act,

(d) your Motion for Default, and Order for Default if your spouse has not responded in the case, and

(e) if there are children, a final Parenting Plan, and an Order of Child Support.

Hand these papers to the bailiff if one is present in the court.

The judge will then motion you to have a seat in the witness box. At this point you may wish to explain that you are representing yourself. You will then testify on the information contained in your Findings of Fact and Decree of Dissolution. You will want to state the following:

(a) Your name and address

(b) Whom you were married to

(c) When and where you were married

(d) That either, or both, of you were resident in Washington when the Petition was filed

(e) That your marriage has irretrievably broken and you can no longer live as husband and wife

(f) That you request the court to terminate your marriage

You would then go on to state how you want the court to settle such matters as matrimonial property and access to the children (naturally this would follow the relief sought in your Petition). For example:

We have X number of children of the marriage. Their names and birthdays are_____.
We have agreed on residential arrangements for the children.

and/or

We have_____
as our debts. Our assets are
_____.

We have agreed that our debts shall be paid by X. Our assets

shall be divided as follows

_____.

These are just rough examples of what you would be expected to say. Before you go to court, you should sit down with a copy of your Petition or your Findings of Fact and draw up brief statements covering each area of relief sought. Then, when you are in court, you can use these notes as a reminder to yourself about what you want to say next. It is not a good idea to read directly from your notes.

The judge will ask you any questions he or she may feel you missed, and then will sign your Decree of Dissolution. You can then thank the court and step down from the witness box.

Now you should take the copies of the papers you brought to court to the county clerk's office. The county clerk will stamp these copies as filed and then will affix the stamp of the judge who signed the originals. In this way you have duplicates of the papers on file in the court. And you have your divorce!

SAMPLE #11
MOTION AND DECLARATION FOR TEMPORARY ORDER (DR 04.0100)

WPF DR 04.0100 (8/91)

SUPERIOR COURT OF WASHINGTON
COUNTY OF SPOKANE

In re the Marriage of:

SUE SNOOPIE,   Petitioner
and
SAM SNOOPIE   Respondent.

NO. 92000

MOTION AND DECLARATION
FOR TEMPORARY ORDER
(MT)

I. MOTION

I move the court for a temporary order granting the following relief:

1.1 TEMPORARY MAINTENANCE.

[X] Does not apply.
[ ] Maintenance should be paid to the [ ] wife [ ] husband in the amount of $ _____ per month.
[ ] Other:

1.2 TEMPORARY SUPPORT FOR THE CHILDREN.

[ ] Does not apply.
[X] Child support should be ordered as determined pursuant to the Washington State Support Schedule.

1.3 PROPOSED TEMPORARY PARENTING PLAN.

[ ] Does not apply.
[X] The temporary parenting plan should be approved which is proposed by the [X] wife [ ] husband [ ] _Sue Snoopie_____.
                                                    (Name)

1.4 TEMPORARY RESTRAINING ORDER.

[ ] Does not apply.
[X] Each party should be restrained from transferring, removing, encumbering, concealing or, in any way disposing of any property except in the usual course of business or for the necessities of life and requiring each party to notify the other of any extraordinary expenditures made after the order is issued.

MOTION FOR TEMPORARY ORDER
RCW 26.09.060; .110; .120; .194
Page 1

WPF DR 04.0100 (8/91)

2 Paragraph 1.4 (continued)

4 [x] Each party should be restrained from molesting or disturbing the peace of the other party or of any child.

6 [x] Each party should be restrained from entering the home of the other party.

8 [x] Each party should be restrained from removing any of the children from the State of Washington.

10 [x] Each party should be restrained from assigning, transferring, borrowing, lapsing, surrendering or changing entitlement of any insurance policies of either or both parties whether medical, health, life or auto insurance.

12

14 [ ] My spouse should be required to surrender any deadly weapon in his or her immediate possession or control or subject to his or her immediate possession or control to the sheriff of the county having jurisdiction of this proceeding, to his or her lawyer or to a person designated by the court. Clear and convincing reasons for this request are set forth in the declaration below. (See RCW 26.09.060(2)(b).)

16

18

20 [ ] Other:

22

1.5 DEBT PAYMENT.

24

[ ] Does not apply.

26 [ ] Each party should be immediately responsible for their own future debts whether incurred by credit card or loan, security interest or mortgage.

28

[x] Responsibility for the debts of the parties should be divided as follows:

30

32

Creditor	Amount of Debt	Responsible Party
Visa	$2,000	Sam Snoopie
Nordstrom	$500	Sue Snoopie
Credit Union Loan	$1,000	Sam Snoopie
SeaFirst Master Card	$200	Sue Snoopie

34

36

38

40

42

MOTION FOR TEMPORARY ORDER
RCW 26.09.060; .110; .120; .194
Page 2

WPF DR 04.0100 (8/91)

2   1.6   PROPERTY.

4   [ ]   Does not apply.
          [X]   The family home should be occupied by the [ ] husband [X] wife.
6   [ ]   The use of other property should be as follows:

8

10

12   1.7   VACATION OF FAMILY HOME.

14   [X]   Does not apply.
          [ ]   My spouse should be ordered to vacate the family home at:
16
           Address:
18

20

       1.8   ATTORNEY'S FEES, OTHER PROFESSIONAL FEES AND COSTS.
22

       [ ]   Does not apply.
24   [X]   The [ ] wife [X] husband should be ordered to pay temporary
             attorney's fees, other professional fees and costs in the amount of
26            $1,000.00 _____ to:

28   the Petitioner

30   1.9   OTHER.

32

This motion is based on the declaration which follows.
34

36   Dated: _2/2/9-_____   _Sue Snoopie_____
                                        Signature of Lawyer or Moving Party (if
38   **moving party has no lawyer)**

40   Sue Snoopie
                                        Print or Type Name (include Washington
42   **State Bar Number, if applicable)**

MOTION FOR TEMPORARY ORDER
RCW 26.09.060; .110; .120; .194
Page 3

WPF DR 04.0100 (8/91)

2

II. DECLARATION

4 It is necessary that the court issue a temporary order granting the relief requested above for the reasons set forth below.

6

2.1   TEMPORARY MAINTENANCE.

8

[X]   Does not apply.

10 [ ]   Maintenance should be paid for the reasons which follow.   A completed financial affidavit accompanies this motion, if required by

12 my county.

14

16

18

20

22

2.2   TEMPORARY SUPPORT FOR THE CHILDREN.

24

[ ]   Does not apply.

26 [X]   Temporary child support should be ordered because there are children who are dependent upon either or both spouses. Completed child

28 support worksheets accompany this motion.

30 2.3   PROPOSED TEMPORARY PARENTING PLAN.

32

[ ]   Does not apply.

[X]   The proposed temporary parenting plan should be approved for the

34 reasons which follow. A Declaration in Support of the Proposed Temporary Parenting Plan accompanies this motion.

36

38

40

42

MOTION FOR TEMPORARY ORDER
RCW 26.09.060; .110; .120; .194
Page 4

WPF DR 04.0100 (8/91)

2   2.4   TEMPORARY RESTRAINING ORDER.

4   [ ]   Does not apply.
        [X]   A temporary restraining order should be issued for the following
6   reasons: Acts of domestic violence on the part of the Respondent/
               father.
8

10

12

14 2.5   DEBT PAYMENT.

16   [X]   Does not apply.
        [ ]   The payment of debts as requested in paragraph 1.5 above should be
18   ordered for the following reasons:

20

22

24

26

2.6   PROPERTY.
28
        [ ]   Does not apply.
30   [X]   The use of property as requested in paragraph 1.6 above should be
               ordered for the following reasons:
32
               I need the family home as a place for the children to live. My
34   husband has left the home.

36

38

40

42

MOTION FOR TEMPORARY ORDER
RCW 26.09.060; .110; .120; .194
Page 5

WPF DR 04.0100 (8/91)

2.7 VACATION OF FAMILY HOME.

[X] Does not apply.
[ ] My spouse should be ordered to vacate the family home for the following reasons:

2.8 ATTORNEY'S FEES, OTHER PROFESSIONAL FEES AND COSTS.

[x] Does not apply.
[ ] The payment of temporary attorney's fees, other professional fees and costs should be ordered for the following reasons:

2.9 OTHER.

I declare under penalty of perjury under the laws of the State of Washington that the foregoing is true and correct.

Signed at ___Spokane, Washington___, on _2/2/9-_.
(City and State)   (Date)

Sue Snoopie
Signature
Sue Snoopie
Print or Type Name and Washington State Bar Number, if applicable

MOTION FOR TEMPORARY ORDER
RCW 26.09.060; .110; .120; .194
Page 6

SAMPLE #12
DECLARATION IN SUPPORT OF PROPOSED
PARENTING PLAN (DR 04.0120)

WPF DR 04.0120 (8/91)

SUPERIOR COURT OF WASHINGTON
COUNTY OF SPOKANE

In re the Marriage of:

SUE SNOOPIE,   Petitioner
and
SAM SNOOPIE,   Respondent.

NO. 92000

DECLARATION IN SUPPORT
OF PROPOSED TEMPORARY
PARENTING PLAN
(DCLR)

(COMPLETE A SEPARATE FORM FOR EACH CHILD IF NECESSARY)

This declaration is made by the [ ] father [X] mother.

1.   _Susie Snoopie_____ has resided with the
                    (Name of Child)
      following persons during the past twelve months:

Name	Address	Length of Time Child Resided With This Person
Sue & Sam Snoopie	North 123 Beagle Street Spokane, WA	all her life

2.   (a)   The mother's performance of parenting functions relating to the daily
             needs of the child during the past twelve months:

             Mother has performed all parenting functions for the child for the
             past six months, and prior to that, provided at least 50 percent
             of the parenting functions.

      (b)   The mother's work schedule for the past twelve months:

             The mother works 9 - 5, Monday through Friday.

      (c)   The mother's current work schedule:
             9 - 5, Monday through Friday.

DECLARATION RE PROPOSED TEMPORARY PLAN
RCW 26.09.194(1)
Page 1

WPF DR 04.0120 (8/91)

2   .3.   (a)   The father's performance of parenting functions relating to the daily needs of the child during the past twelve months:

4   p   None during the past six months. Less than 50 percent prior to that time.

6

8   (b)   The father's work schedule for the past twelve months:

     Unknown.

10

12

       (c)   The father's current work schedule:

14   Unknown.

16

18   4.   (a)   The child-care schedule for the past twelve months:

     Child has been in a day care from 8:30 a.m. to 5:30 p.m., Monday

20   through Friday for the past twelve months.

22

       (b)   The current child-care schedule:

24   Same as above.

26

28   5.   Any circumstances under RCW 26.09.191 that are likely to pose a serious risk to the child(ren) and that warrant limitation on the award to a parent

30   of temporary residence or time with the child(ren) pending entry of a permanent parenting plan are set forth in Part II of my proposed temporary

32   parenting plan.

34   I declare under penalty of perjury under the laws of the State of Washington that the foregoing is true and correct.

36

Signed at ___Spokane, Washington_____, on _2/2/9-___.

38   (City and State)   (Date)

                                      Sue Snoopie

40   Signature

                             Sue Snoopie

42   Print or Type Name

DECLARATION RE PROPOSED TEMPORARY PLAN
RCW 26.09.194(1)
Page 2

WPF DR 04.0250 (8/91)

SUPERIOR COURT OF WASHINGTON
COUNTY OF SPOKANE

In re the Marriage of:

SUE SNOOPIE,   Petitioner

and

SAM SNOOPIE   Respondent.

NO. 92000

TEMPORARY ORDER
(TMO)
[ ] CLERK'S ACTION REQUIRED
(See Paragraph 2.10)

I. JUDGMENT SUMMARY

A. Judgment Creditor ___Sue Snoopie___
B. Judgment Debtor ___Sam Snoopie___
C. Principal judgment amount (back support) $ ___500___
from April 199- to May 199-.
   (Date)   (Date)
D. Interest to date of Judgment . . . .$ ___none___
E. Attorney's fees. . . . .$ ___none___
F. Costs . . . .$ _____
G. Other recovery amount. . . . . $ _____
H. Principal judgment shall bear interest at ___12___ % per annum.
I. Attorney's fees, costs and other recovery
amounts shall bear interest at . . . . . _____ % per annum.
J. Attorney for Judgment Creditor ___none___
K. Attorney for Judgment Debtor ___none___

II. ORDER

It is ORDERED that:

2.1 RESTRAINING ORDER.

[ ] Does not apply.
[X] Each party is restrained from assaulting, harassing, molesting or disturbing the peace of the other party.*
[X] Each party is restrained from entering the home of the other party.*

*VIOLATION OF THE ABOVE PROVISIONS OF THIS ORDER WITH ACTUAL NOTICE OF THEIR TERMS IS A CRIMINAL OFFENSE UNDER CHAPTER 26.09 RCW, AND WILL SUBJECT THE VIOLATOR TO ARREST. RCW 26.09.060.

TEMPORARY ORDER ALL ISSUES
RCW 26.09.060; .110; .120; .194
Page 1

SAMPLE #13 — Continued

WPF DR 04.0250 (8/91)

2 | Paragraph 2.1 (continued)

4   [X] Each party is restrained from assigning, transferring, borrowing, lapsing, surrendering, or changing entitlements of any insurance
6   policy of either party whether medical, health, life or auto insurance.

8   [x] Each party is restrained from transferring, removing, encumbering, concealing, or in any way disposing of any assets
10   including retirement, profit sharing, or similar accounts except in the usual order of business or for the necessities of life;

12   [x] Each party is restrained from molesting or disturbing the peace of the other by telephone or otherwise at his or her
14   employment.

  [x] Each party shall be personally responsible for any indebtedness
16   incurred by that person whether by credit card or loan, security interest or mortgage, commencing with the date of this order.

18   [X] Each party is restrained from removing any of the children from the jurisdiction (State of Washington) of this court, without further court
20   order except for vacation or visitation.

  [ ] Other:

22

24

26

28

30 | 2.2   SURRENDER OF DEADLY WEAPONS.

32   [X] Does not apply.
  [ ] It is ordered that _____ surrender
34   (Name)
any deadly weapon in his or her immediate possession or control or
36   subject to his or her immediate possession or control to:

38   [ ] the _____ county sheriff.
(Name of County)
40   [ ] _____.
(Name)
42

TEMPORARY ORDER ALL ISSUES
RCW 26.09.060; .110; .120; .194
Page 2

88

WPF DR 04.0250 (8/91)

2 2.3 PARENTING PLAN.

4 [ ] Does not apply.
   [X] The parties shall comply with the attached Temporary Parenting Plan
6 signed by the court. The attached Temporary Parenting Plan signed
   by the court is approved and incorporated as part of this order.

8
   2.4 CHILD SUPPORT.
10
   [ ] Does not apply.
12 [X] Child support shall be paid in accordance with the attached order of
   child support, signed by the court, which is incorporated as part of
14 this temporary order.

16 2.5 SPOUSAL MAINTENANCE.

18 [X] Does not apply.
   [ ] The [ ] husband [ ] wife shall pay the other $ _____ per
20 month maintenance.

22 Starting Date:
   Day(s) of the month payment is due:
24
   Payments shall be made to:
26
   [ ] the Washington state support registry (if child support is
28 ordered).
   [ ] directly to the other spouse.
30 [ ] the clerk of this court as trustee for remittance to the other
   spouse (if there are no dependent children).
32
   2.6 APPOINTMENT OF CHILD'S GAL/INVESTIGATOR/LAWYER.
34
   [X] Does not apply.
36 [ ] The motion for the appointment of a [ ] lawyer [ ] investigator
   [ ] guardian ad litem for the child(ren) is denied.
38 [ ] The motion for the appointment of a [ ] lawyer [ ] investigator
   [ ] guardian ad litem for the child(ren) is granted. A separate order
40 setting forth the duties of this person has been or will be entered by
   the court.
42

TEMPORARY ORDER ALL ISSUES
RCW 26.09.060; .110; .120; .194
Page 3

WPF DR 04.0250 (8/91)

2   2.7   REAL PROPERTY.

4   [ ]   Does not apply.
     [}   The family home located at North 123 Beagle Street, Spokane, WA
6   (Address)
            shall be occupied by the [ ] husband [X] wife.
8   [ ]   Use of other real property shall be as follows:

10

12

14

16

18

20

22

24   2.8   PERSONAL PROPERTY.

26   The use of the personal property of the parties shall be as follows:

28   The wife shall have exclusive use of the 1990 Buick.

30

32

34

36

38

40

42

TEMPORARY ORDER ALL ISSUES
RCW 26.09.060; .110; .120; .194
Page 4

WPF DR 04.0250 (8/91)

2   2.9   ATTORNEY'S FEES, OTHER PROFESSIONAL FEES AND COSTS.

4   [X]   Does not apply.
          [ ]   The [ ] husband [ ] wife is awarded $ _____ temporary
6   attorney's fees, $ _____ for other professional fees and
                 $ _____ costs, payable by the other party.
8

   2.10   CLERK'S ACTION/LAW ENFORCEMENT ACTION.
10

12   [ ]   Does not apply.
          [X]   This order shall be filed forthwith in the clerk's office and entered of
                 record.
14

16   The clerk of the court shall forward a copy of this order on or before
                 the next judicial day, to Spokane County Sheriff _____.
18   (Name of law enforcement agency)

20   _____ shall forthwith enter this order
                 (Name of law enforcement agency)
                 into any computer-based criminal intelligence system available in this
22   state used by law enforcement agencies to list outstanding warrants.

24   2.11   OTHER:

26

28   **THIS IS A TEMPORARY ORDER PENDING FURTHER ORDER OF THE**
   COURT, REQUIRING COMPLIANCE WITH THE RESTRAINING ORDERS
30   **AND PARAGRAPHS ABOVE.**

32

   Dated: January 10, 199- _____   *JM Commissioner*
34   Judge/Commissioner

36   Presented by: Approved for entry:
                                      Notice of presentation waived:
38

40   *Sue Snoopie*
   Signature and Washington State Bar   Signature and Washington State Bar
42   Number, if applicable   Number, if applicable
   Sue Snoopie, Petitioner

   TEMPORARY ORDER ALL ISSUES
   RCW 26.09.060; .110; .120; .194
   Page 5

WPF DR 01.0300 (7/91)

SUPERIOR COURT OF WASHINGTON
COUNTY OF SPOKANE

NO.   92000

In re the Marriage of:

SUE SNOOPIE,   Petitioner

RESPONSE TO PETITION
(DOMESTIC RELATIONS)
(RSP) or (JN)

and
SAM SNOOPIE,   Respondent.

TO THE ABOVE-NAMED PETITIONER:

1.   AGREEMENT AND JOINDER.

　　[X]   I do not agree with or join in the petition.
　　[ ]   I AGREE with the relief requested in the petition and JOIN in the
　　　　　petition. I understand that by joining in the petition, I am waiving
　　　　　any objections I might have to the allegations of the petition and that
　　　　　the relief requested in the petition will be granted and judgment
　　　　　entered. I also understand that paragraphs 2, 3 and 4 below do not
　　　　　apply.

　　[ ]   I waive notice of all further proceedings in this matter.
　　[ ]   I demand notice of all further proceedings in this matter.
　　　　　Further notice should be sent to me at the following address:

2.   ADMISSIONS AND DENIALS.

　　[ ]   Does not apply.
　　[X]   The allegations of the petition in this matter are ADMITTED or
　　　　　DENIED as follows (check only one for each paragraph):

RESPONSE TO PETITION
RCW 4.28.010; 26.09.010
Page 1

WPF DR 01.0300 (7/91)

2 | Paragraph 2 (continued)

4

Paragraph of the Petition	Admitted	Denied
1.1	X	
1.2	X	
1.3	X	
1.4	X	
1.5	X	
1.6	X	
1.7		X
1.8	X	
1.9	X	
1.10		X
1.11	X	
1.12	X	
1.13		
1.14		X

The allegations of the petition which are denied, are denied for the following reasons:

not necessary and not good pleading

RESPONSE TO PETITION
RCW 4.28.010; 26.09.010
Page 2

WPF DR 01.0300 (7/91)

3.   REQUEST FOR RELIEF.

[ ]   Does not apply.
[x]   I REQUEST the Court to grant the relief requested below.

[ ]   Provide reasonable maintenance for the [ ] husband [ ] wife.
[ ]   Approve my parenting plan for the dependent children.
[ ]   Determine support for the dependent children pursuant to the Washington State Support Schedule.
[ ]   Approve the separation agreement.
[X]   Dispose of property and liabilities.
[ ]   Change name of wife to: _____.
[ ]   Change name of husband to: _____.
[ ]   Enter a permanent restraining order.
[ ]   Order payment of day care expenses for the children.
[X]   Award the tax exemptions for the dependent children as follows:
        to the Respondent

[ ]   Order payment of attorney's fees, other professional fees and costs.

4.   Other:

Dated: _February 10, 199-_____   *Sam Snoopie*
                                         Signature of Lawyer or Respondent (if respondent has no lawyer)
                                         Sam Snoopie

                                         Print or Type Name (include Washington State Bar Number, if applicable)

I declare under penalty of perjury under the laws of the State of Washington that the foregoing is true and correct.

Signed at _Yakima, Washington_____, on _2/10/9-___.
              (City and State)   (Date)
                          Sam Snoopie
                              Signature
                          Sam Snoopie
                          Print or Type Name

RESPONSE TO PETITION
RCW 4.28.010; 26.09.010
Page 3

WPF DR 04.0300 (8/91)

SUPERIOR COURT OF WASHINGTON
COUNTY OF SPOKANE

In re the Marriage of:

SUE SNOOPIE,   Petitioner

and

SAM SNOOPIE,   Respondent.

NO. 92000

**FINDINGS OF FACT AND
CONCLUSIONS OF LAW
(FNFCL)**

I. HEARING/TRIAL

1.1   A hearing was held on <u>April 12, 199-</u> .
                                    (Date)

1.2   The findings are based on:

    [ ]   trial.
    [ ]   agreement.
    [X]   an order of default entered on <u>April 12, 199-</u> .
                                                    (Date)

1.3   The following people attended:

    [X]   Petitioner:
    [ ]   Petitioner's Lawyer:
    [ ]   Respondent:
    [ ]   Respondent's Lawyer:
    [ ]   Other:

II. FINDINGS OF FACT

Upon the basis of the court record, the court FINDS:

2.1   The petitioner is a resident of the State of Washington or is a member of
        the armed forces and is stationed in this state.

2.2   The court has subject matter jurisdiction over the marriage. The respondent

    [ ]   appeared or responded.
    [X]   was served in the following manner:
                Personally served on the Respondent

FINDINGS OF FACT AND CONCLUSIONS OF LAW
CR 52; RCW 26.09.030; .070(3)
Page 1

WPF DR 04.0300 (8/91)

2   2.3   BASIS OF JURISDICTION OVER THE RESPONDENT.

4   [ ]   There are no facts to establish personal jurisdiction over the respondent.

6   [X]   The facts below establish personal jurisdiction over the respondent.

8   [x]   The respondent is presently residing in Washington.

             [ ]   The parties lived in Washington during their marriage and the

10   petitioner continues to reside in this state.

             [ ]   The parties lived in Washington during their marriage and the

12   petitioner continues to be a member of the armed forces stationed in this state.

14   [ ]   The parties may have conceived a child while within Washington.

16   [ ]   The respondent was served within the State of Washington.

             [ ]   The petitioner resides in Washington and the respondent

18   consents to jurisdiction.

             [ ]   Other:

20

    2.4   The parties were married on <u>July 2, 1980</u> at <u>Seattle, Washington</u>.

22   (Date)   (Place)

24   2.5   STATUS OF THE PARTIES.

26   [ ]   Husband and wife are not separated.

        [X]   Husband and wife separated on <u>March 1, 1988</u>.

28   (Date)

30   2.6   STATUS OF THE MARRIAGE.

32   [x]   The marriage is irretrievably broken and at least 90 days have elapsed

                 since the date the petition was filed and since the date the summons

34   was served or the respondent joined.

        [ ]   The petitioner wishes to be legally separated.

36   [ ]   The petitioner is petitioning for a declaration concerning the invalidity

                 of the marriage. The court FINDS the following facts concerning the

38   validity of the marriage:

40

42

FINDINGS OF FACT AND CONCLUSIONS OF LAW
CR 52; RCW 26.09.030; .070(3)
Page 2

WPF DR 04.0300 (8/91)

2 2.7   SEPARATION CONTRACT.

4   [X]   There is no written separation contract or prenuptial agreement.
      [ ]   A written separation contract or prenuptial agreement was executed
6   on _____ and is filed herein.
                  (Date)
8
             [ ]   The separation contract [ ] was [ ] was not fair when executed.
10   [ ]   The separation contract [ ] should [ ] should not be approved.

12 2.8   COMMUNITY PROPERTY.

14   [ ]   The parties do not have community property.
      [ ]   The parties have community property as set forth in Exhibit ___.
16   This exhibit is attached or filed and incorporated by reference as part
             of these findings.
18   [X]   The parties have the following community property:
             A house at North 123 Beagle Street, Spokane, Washington
20   1990 Taurus car
             Bank accounts
22   The furniture in the family home
             Wife's pension at Acme Widget Co.
24   Husband's pension at XYZ Corp.
             1985 Buick
26

28

30

32

34

36

38

40

42

FINDINGS OF FACT AND CONCLUSIONS OF LAW
CR 52; RCW 26.09.030; .070(3)
Page 3

WPF DR 04.0300 (8/91)

2   2.9   HUSBAND'S SEPARATE PROPERTY.

4   [x]   The husband has no separate property.
       [ ]   The husband has separate property as set forth in Exhibit ___. This
6   exhibit is attached or filed and incorporated by reference as part of
            these findings.
8   [ ]   The husband has the following separate property:

24 2.10 WIFE'S SEPARATE PROPERTY.

26   [X]   The wife has no separate property.
       [ ]   The wife has separate property as set forth in Exhibit ___. This
28   exhibit is attached or filed and incorporated by reference as part of
           these findings.
30   [ ]   The wife has the following separate property:

FINDINGS OF FACT AND CONCLUSIONS OF LAW
CR 52; RCW 26.09.030; .070(3)
Page 4

98

WPF DR 04.0300 (8/91)

2.11 COMMUNITY DEBTS AND OTHER LIABILITIES.

[ ] There are no known community obligations.
[ ] The parties have incurred community debts and liabilities as set forth in Exhibit ___. This exhibit is attached or filed and incorporated by reference as part of these findings.
[X] The parties have incurred the following community debts and liabilities:

Creditor	Amount
Visa	$2,000
Nordstrom	$500
Credit Union Loan	$1,000
SeaFirst MasterCard	$200

2.12 HUSBAND'S SEPARATE DEBTS AND OTHER LIABILITIES.

[x] The husband has no known separate obligations.
[ ] The husband has incurred separate debts and liabilities as set forth in Exhibit ___. This exhibit is attached or filed and incorporated by reference as part of these findings.
[ ] The husband has incurred the following separate debts and liabilities:

Creditor	Amount

FINDINGS OF FACT AND CONCLUSIONS OF LAW
CR 52; RCW 26.09.030; .070(3)
Page 5

WPF DR 04.0300 (8/91)

2   2.13   WIFE'S SEPARATE DEBTS AND OTHER LIABILITIES.

4   [X]   The wife has no known separate obligations.
         [ ]   The wife has incurred separate debts and liabilities as set forth
6   in Exhibit ___. This exhibit is attached or filed and incorporated by
                reference as part of these findings.
8   [ ]   The wife has incurred the following separate debts and liabilities:

10   Creditor   Amount

26
·   2.14   NEED FOR MAINTENANCE.
28
         [X]   Neither party is in need of maintenance.
30   [ ]   The [ ] husband [ ] wife is in need of spousal maintenance. This
                finding is based upon the following factors:
32
                [ ]   The party seeking maintenance is unable to meet his or her
34   needs independently.
                [ ]   The time necessary to acquire sufficient education or training
36   to enable the party seeking maintenance to find employment
                       appropriate to his or her skill, interests, style of life and other
38   attendant circumstances.
                [ ]   The standard of living established during the marriage.
40   [ ]   The duration of the marriage.
                [ ]   The age, physical and emotional condition, and financial
42   obligations of the party seeking maintenance.

FINDINGS OF FACT AND CONCLUSIONS OF LAW
CR 52; RCW 26.09.030; .070(3)
Page 6

WPF DR 04.0300 (8/91)

2   Paragraph 2.14 (continued)

4   [ ]   The past, present and future earning or economic capacity of each spouse, including the earning or economic capacity of
6   each spouse that was enhanced, diminished or foregone during the marriage.
8   [ ]   The standard of living each spouse will experience after dissolution of the marriage.
10   [ ]   The ability of the spouse from whom maintenance is sought to meet his or her needs and financial obligations while meeting
12   those of the spouse seeking maintenance.
          [ ]   A lack of work history, education or training.
14   [ ]   Other:

16

    2.15   ABILITY TO PAY MAINTENANCE.
18

20   [X]   Does not apply.
       [ ]   The [ ] husband   [ ] wife has the ability to pay maintenance as follows:
22

24

26

28

30   2.16   RESTRAINING ORDER.

32   [X]   Does not apply.
       [ ]   A continuing restraining order against the [ ] husband [ ] wife
34   [ ] both parties is necessary because:

36

38

40

42

FINDINGS OF FACT AND CONCLUSIONS OF LAW
CR 52; RCW 26.09.030; .070(3)
Page 7

WPF DR 04.0300 (8/91)

2 2.17 COURT COSTS AND FEES.

4 [x] Does not apply.
   [ ] The following court costs and fees have been incurred in this action:

6

8

10

12

14

   2.18 ATTORNEY'S FEES AND COSTS.

16

   [X] Does not apply.
18 [ ] Each of the parties has sufficient property, income or resources
        available to pay his or her own respective attorney fees and costs.
20 [ ] The [ ] husband [ ] wife has incurred reasonable attorney fees and
        costs in the amount of $ _____. The other spouse has the ability
22   to pay these fees and the [ ] husband [ ] wife has the need for the
        payment of these fees as follows:

24

26

28

30

32 2.19 PREGNANCY.

34 [X] The wife is not pregnant.
    [ ] The wife is pregnant. The father of the unborn child is [ ] the
36   husband [ ] not the husband [ ] unknown.

38 2.20 DEPENDENT CHILDREN.

40 [ ] The parties have no dependent children.
    [X] The parties have children who are dependent or partially dependent
42   upon either or both spouses.

FINDINGS OF FACT AND CONCLUSIONS OF LAW
CR 52; RCW 26.09.030; .070(3)
Page 8

102

WPF DR 04.0300 (8/91)

2 2.21 JURISDICTION OVER THE CHILDREN.

4 [ ] Does not apply.
   [ ] This court does not have jurisdiction over the children.
6 [X] This court has jurisdiction over the children for the reasons set forth below.

8
   [X] This state is the home state of the child because
10
       [X] the child lived in Washington with a parent or a person
12   acting as a parent for at least six consecutive months
             immediately preceding the commencement of this
14   proceeding.
       [ ] the child is less than six months old and has lived in
16   Washington with a parent or a person acting as parent
             since birth.
18   [ ] any absences from Washington have been only
             temporary.
20   [ ] Washington was the home state of the child within six
             months before the commencement of this proceeding
22   and the child's absence from the state is because of
             removal or retention by a person claiming custody or for
24   other reasons.

26   [ ] It is in the best interest of the child that this court assume
          jurisdiction because the child and the parents or the child and
28   at least one contestant have significant connection with the
          state; there is substantial evidence concerning the child's
30   present or future care, protection, training and personal
          relationships in the state; and
32
       [ ] the child has no home state elsewhere.
34   [ ] the child's home state has declined to exercise
             jurisdiction.
36
     [ ] The child is physically present in this state and has been
38   abandoned or it is necessary in an emergency to protect the
          child because he or she has been subjected to or threatened
40   with mistreatment or abuse.

42

FINDINGS OF FACT AND CONCLUSIONS OF LAW
CR 52; RCW 26.09.030; .070(3)
Page 9

WPF DR 04.0300 (8/91)

2 | Paragraph 2.21 (continued)

4 | [ ]   No other state has jurisdiction or a state with jurisdiction has declined to exercise jurisdiction on the ground that this state

6 | is the more appropriate forum and it is in the best interest of the child for this court to assume jurisdiction.

8 | [ ]   This court has continuing jurisdiction because the court has previously made a child custody or parenting plan

10 | determination in this matter and Washington remains the residence of the children or any contestant.

12 | [ ]   Other:

14 |

16 |

2.24 PARENTING PLAN.

18 |

[ ]   Does not apply.

20 | [x]   The attached or filed Parenting Plan signed by the court is approved and incorporated as part of these findings.

22 |

2.25 CHILD SUPPORT.

24 |

[ ]   Does not apply.

26 | [x]   There are children in need of support and child support should be set pursuant to the Washington State Child Support Schedule.

28 |

2.26 OTHER:

30 |

32 |

34 |

36 |

38 |

40 |

42 |

FINDINGS OF FACT AND CONCLUSIONS OF LAW
CR 52; RCW 26.09.030; .070(3)
Page 10

WPF DR 04.0300 (8/91)

2   III. CONCLUSIONS OF LAW

4   The court makes the following conclusions of law from the foregoing findings of
fact:

6   3.1   The court has jurisdiction over the:

8
        [X]   parties
10   [X]   subject matter
        [ ]   property and obligations

12   3.2   The parties should be granted a decree:

14
        [X]   of dissolution.
16   [ ]   of legal separation.
        [ ]   declaring the marriage invalid.
18   [ ]   declaring the marriage valid.

20
3.3   The court has disposed of the property, liabilities, fees, costs, made a
22   parenting plan and provision for support of the child(ren), if any, and
        maintenance, if any, all in an equitable manner.

24   3.4   PROPERTY TO BE AWARDED THE HUSBAND.

26
        [ ]   Does not apply.
28   [ ]   The husband should be awarded as his separate property the property
               set forth in Exhibit _____. This exhibit is attached or filed and
30   incorporated by reference as part of these findings.
        [X]   The husband should be awarded as his separate property the following
32   property (list real estate, furniture, vehicles, pensions, insurance, bank
               accounts, etc.):

34   His pension at XYZ Corp.
                   1985 Buick
36   His Bank account

38

40

42

FINDINGS OF FACT AND CONCLUSIONS OF LAW
CR 52; RCW 26.09.030; .070(3)
Page 11

WPF DR 04.0300 (8/91)

2 3.5 PROPERTY TO BE AWARDED TO THE WIFE.

4 [ ] Does not apply.
  [ ] The wife should be awarded as her separate property the property
6   set forth in Exhibit ____. This exhibit is attached or filed and
    incorporated by reference as part of these findings.
8 [X] The wife should be awarded as her separate property the following
    property (list real estate, furniture, vehicles, pensions, insurance, bank
10   accounts, etc.):

12   A house at North 123 beagle Street, Spokane, washington

      1990 Taurus car
      Her bank accounts
14   The furniture in the family home
      Her pension at Acme Widget Co.

22

3.6 OBLIGATIONS TO BE PAID BY THE HUSBAND.
24

  [ ] Does not apply.
26 [ ] The husband should pay the community or separate obligations as set
    forth in Exhibit ____. This exhibit is attached or filed and
28   incorporated by reference as part of these findings.
  [X] The husband should pay the following community or separate
30   obligations:

32

Creditor	Amount
Visa	$2,000
Credit Union Loan	$1,000

FINDINGS OF FACT AND CONCLUSIONS OF LAW
CR 52; RCW 26.09.030; .070(3)
Page 12

WPF DR 04.0300 (8/91)

3.7 OBLIGATIONS TO BE PAID BY THE WIFE.

[ ] Does not apply.
[ ] The wife should pay the community or separate obligations as set forth in Exhibit _____. This exhibit is attached or filed and incorporated by reference as part of these findings.
[X] The wife should pay the following community or separate obligations:

Creditor	Amount
Nordstrom	$500
SeaFirst MasterCard	$200

3.8 NAME CHANGES.

[ ] Does not apply.
[X] The wife's name should be changed to ___Sue Smith___.
(Name)

[ ] The husband's name should be changed to _____.
(Name)

3.9 RESTRAINING ORDER.

[ ] Does not apply.
[X] A continuing restraining order should be entered as follows:

The Respondent/father is restained from molesting or disturbing the peace of the other party or of any child.

FINDINGS OF FACT AND CONCLUSIONS OF LAW
CR 52; RCW 26.09.030; .070(3)
Page 13

WPF DR 04.0300 (8/91)

2 3.10 ATTORNEY'S FEES AND COSTS.

4 [x] Does not apply.
   [ ] Attorney's fees, other professional fees and costs should be paid as
6   follows:

8

10

12 3.11 OTHER:

14

16

18

20

22

24

26

28

30

32

Dated: ___April 12, 199-___   *J. M. Commissioner*
34   Judge/Commissioner

36 Presented by: Approved for entry:
                                       Notice of presentation waived:
38

40 *Sue Snoopie*
    _____   _____
    Signature and Washington State Bar   Signature and Washington State Bar
42 Number, if applicable   Number, if applicable
    Sue Snoopie
    FINDINGS OF FACT AND CONCLUSIONS OF LAW
    CR 52; RCW 26.09.030; .070(3)
    Page 14

SAMPLE #16
DECREE OF DISSOLUTION (DR 04.0400)

WPF DR 04.0400 (8/91)

**SUPERIOR COURT OF WASHINGTON
COUNTY OF** SPOKANE

In re the Marriage of:

SUE SNOOPIE,   Petitioner

and

SAM SNOOPIE,   Respondent.

NO. 92000
DECREE OF DISSOLUTION/
LEGAL SEPARATION/
CONCERNING VALIDITY
(DCD) or (DCLGSP) or (DCINMG)
[ ] CLERK'S ACTION REQUIRED
(See paragraph 3.11)

I. JUDGMENT SUMMARY

A. Judgment Creditor _____
B. Judgment Debtor _____
C. Principal judgment amount (back support) $ _____
   from _____ to _____.
        (Date)   (Date)
D. Interest to date of Judgment . . . . $ _____
E. Attorney's fees . . . . $ _____
F. Costs . . . . $ _____
G. Other recovery amount. . . . . $ _____
H. Principal judgment shall bear interest at _____% per annum.
I. Attorney's fees, costs and other recovery
   amounts shall bear interest at . . . . . . _____% per annum.
J. Attorney for Judgment Creditor _____
K. Attorney for Judgment Debtor _____

II. BASIS

The findings of fact and conclusions of law have been entered in this case.

III. DECREE

IT IS DECREED that:

3.1 STATUS OF THE MARRIAGE.

   [x]   The marriage of the parties is dissolved.
   [ ]   The husband and wife are legally separated.
   [ ]   The marriage of the parties is invalid as of _____.
                              (Date)
   [ ]   The marriage of the parties is valid.

DECREE
RCW 26.09.030; .040; .070(3)
Page 1

WPF DR 04.0400 (8/91)

2   3.2   PARENTING PLAN.

4   [ ]   Does not apply.
          [X]   The parties shall comply with the Parenting Plan signed by the court,
6   which is attached or filed. The Parenting Plan signed by the court is
                 approved and incorporated as part of this decree.

8

     3.3   CHILD SUPPORT.

10
          [ ]   Does not apply.
12   [x]   Child support shall be paid in accordance with the order of child
                 support signed by the court, which is attached or filed.   This order
14   is incorporated as part of this decree.

16   3.4   PROPERTY TO BE AWARDED THE HUSBAND.

18   [ ]   Does not apply.
          [ ]   The husband is awarded as his separate property the property set
20   forth in Exhibit _____.   This exhibit is attached or filed and
                 incorporated by reference as part of this decree.
22   [x]   The husband is awarded as his separate property the following
                 property (list real estate, furniture, vehicles, pensions, insurance, bank
24   accounts, etc.):
                      His pension at XYZ Corp.
26   1985 Buick
                      His bank account

28

30

32

34

36

38

40

42

DECREE
RCW 26.09.030; .040; .070(3)
Page 2

WPF DR 04.0400 (8/91)

2 3.5 PROPERTY TO BE AWARDED TO THE WIFE.

4 [ ] Does not apply.
   [ ] The wife is awarded as her separate property the property set forth
6   in Exhibit ___. This exhibit is attached or filed and incorporated by
        reference as part of this decree.
8 [x] The wife is awarded as her separate property the following property
        (list real estate, furniture, vehicles, pensions, insurance, bank accounts,
10   etc.):

12   A house at North 123 Beagle Street

        1990 Taurus car
14   Her bank accounts
        The furniture in the family home
16   Her pension at Acme Widget Co.

18

20

22

24

26

28

30

32

34

36

38

40

42

DECREE
RCW 26.09.030; .040; .070(3)
Page 3

WPF DR 04.0400 (8/91)

3.6 OBLIGATIONS TO BE PAID BY THE HUSBAND.

[ ] Does not apply.

[ ] The husband shall pay the community or separate obligations set forth in Exhibit _____. This exhibit is attached or filed and incorporated by reference as part of this decree.

[x] The husband shall pay the following community or separate obligations:

Creditor	Amount
Visa	$2,000
Credit Union Loan	$1,000

DECREE
RCW 26.09.030; .040; .070(3)
Page 4

WPF DR 04.0400 (8/91)

2   3.7   OBLIGATIONS TO BE PAID BY THE WIFE.

4   [ ]   Does not apply.
    [ ]   The wife shall pay the community or separate obligations set forth
6   in Exhibit ___. This exhibit is attached or filed and incorporated by
          reference as part of this decree.
8   [x]   The wife shall pay the following community or separate obligations:

10   Creditor   Amount
                          Nordstrom $500
12   SeaFirst MasterCard $200

14

16

18

20

22

24

26

28

30

32

34

    3.8   HOLD HARMLESS PROVISION.
36
    [ ]   Does not apply.
38 [x]   Each party is required to pay all debt incurred since the date of
          separation and to hold the other party harmless from any collection
40   action relating to separate or community debt, including reasonable
          attorney's fees and costs incurred in defending against any attempts
42   to collect an obligation of the other party.

DECREE
RCW 26.09.030; .040; .070(3)
Page 5

113

WPF DR 04.0400 (8/91)

2   3.9   SPOUSAL MAINTENANCE.

4   [X]   Does not apply.

            [ ]   The [ ] husband [ ] wife shall pay maintenance as set forth in Exhibit

6   ____. This exhibit is attached or filed and incorporated by reference as part of this decree.

8   [ ]   The [ ] husband [ ] wife shall pay $ _____ maintenance. Maintenance shall be paid [ ] weekly [ ] semi-monthly [ ] monthly.

10   The first maintenance payment shall be due on _____. The

                                                   (Date)

12   obligation to pay future maintenance is terminated:

14   [ ]   upon the death of either party or the remarriage of the party receiving maintenenance.

16   [ ]   Other:

18

20

                Payments shall be made:

22

            [ ]   directly to the other spouse.

24   [ ]   to the Washington State Support Registry (only available if child support is ordered).

26   [ ]   to the clerk of this court as trustee for remittance to the other spouse (only available if there are no dependent children).

28

       [ ]   If a spousal maintenance payment is more than fifteen days past due

30   and the total of such past due payments is equal to or greater than one hundred dollars, or if the obligor requests a withdrawal of

32   accumulated contributions from the Department of Retirement Systems, the obligee may seek a mandatory benefits assignment order

34   under Chapter 41.50 RCW without prior notice to the obligor.

       [ ]   The Department of Retirement Systems may make a direct payment

36   of all or part of a withdrawal of accumulated contributions pursuant to RCW 41.50.550(3).

38   [ ]   Other:

40

42

DECREE
RCW 26.09.030; .040; .070(3)
Page 6

WPF DR 04.0400 (8/91)

2 3.10 NAME CHANGES.

4 [ ] Does not apply.
   [X] The wife's name shall be changed to ___Sue Smith___.
6   (Name)
   [ ] The husband's name shall be changed to _____.
8   (Name)

10 3.11 CONTINUING RESTRAINING ORDER.

12 [ ] Does not apply.
    [X] A continuing restraining order is entered as follows:

14
    [X] Each party is restrained from assaulting, harassing, molesting
16   or disturbing the peace of the other party.*
    [ ] Each party is restrained from entering the home of the other
18   party.*

20   ***VIOLATION OF THE ABOVE PROVISIONS OF THIS
         ORDER WITH ACTUAL NOTICE OF THEIR TERMS IS A
22   CRIMINAL OFFENSE UNDER CHAPTER 26.09 RCW, AND
         WILL SUBJECT THE VIOLATOR TO ARREST. RCW
24   26.09.060.**
    [ ] Other:
26

28

30

         This order shall be filed forthwith in the clerk's office and entered of
32   record.

34   The clerk of the court shall forward a copy of this order on or before
         the next judicial day, to _Spokane County Sheriff's Dept._
36   (Name of law enforcement agency)

38 _Spokane County Sheriff's Dept_ shall forthwith enter this order
    (Name of law enforcement agency)
40   into any computer-based criminal intelligence system available in this
         state used by law enforcement agencies to list outstanding warrants.
42

DECREE
RCW 26.09.030; .040; .070(3)
Page 7

WPF DR 04.0400 (8/91)

2   3.12   ATTORNEY'S FEES, OTHER PROFESSIONAL FEES AND COSTS.

4   [X]   Does not apply.

      [ ]   Attorney's fees, other professional fees and costs shall be paid as

6   follows:

8

10

12

14

3.13   OTHER:

16

18

20

22

24

26

28

30

32

Dated: ___April 12, 199-___   *J. M. Commissioner*

34   Judge/Commissioner

36   Presented by: Approved for entry:

                                  Notice of presentation waived:

38

40   *Sue Snoopie*

   Signature and Washington State Bar   Signature and Washington State Bar

42   Number, if applicable   Number, if applicable

     Sue Snoopie

     Petitioner

DECREE

RCW 26.09.030; .040; .070(3)

Page 8

WPF DR 01.0500 (8/91)

SUPERIOR COURT OF WASHINGTON
COUNTY OF SPOKANE

In re:

SUE SNOOPIE,   Petitioner

and

SAM SNOOPIE,   Respondent.

NO.   92000

ORDER OF CHILD SUPPORT
(ORS)

I. JUDGMENT SUMMARY

A.   Judgment Creditor _____

B.   Judgment Debtor _____

C.   Principal judgment amount (back support) $ _____
      from _____ to _____.
            (Date)   (Date)

D.   Interest to date of Judgment . . . .$ _____

E.   Attorney's fees . . . .$ _____

F.   Costs . . . . $ _____

G.   Other recovery amount. . . . . $ _____

H.   Principal judgment shall bear interest at _____% per annum.

I.   Attorney's fees, costs and other recovery
      amounts shall bear interest at . . . . . _____% per annum.

J.   Attorney for Judgment Creditor _____

K.   Attorney for Judgment Debtor _____

II. BASIS

2.1   This order is entered pursuant to a:

      [X]   decree of dissolution, legal separation or a declaration of invalidity.
      [ ]   finding of parentage.
      [ ]   petition for modification of child support.
      [ ]   temporary order.
      [ ]   other:

2.2   The child support worksheet(s) which are initialed by the court are attached
      or filed and are incorporated by reference.

ORDER OF CHILD SUPPORT
RCW 26.09.175; 26.26.132(5)
Page 1

WPF DR 01.0500 (8/91)

III. ORDER

IT IS ORDERED that:

3.1 CHILDREN FOR WHOM SUPPORT IS REQUIRED.

Name	Date of Birth	Soc. Sec. Number
Susie Snoopie	1/10/82	001-20-3333

3.2 PERSON PAYING SUPPORT (OBLIGOR).

Name: Sam Snoopie
Address: East 6000 - 14th Ave., Yakima, WA 98093

Soc.Sec.Num: 123-00-5678
Employer and Address: XYZ Corp.

[x] Monthly Net Income: $ 1,000 _____
[ ] The income of the obligor is imputed at $ _____
   because:

    [ ] the obligor's income is unknown.
    [ ] the obligor is voluntarily unemployed.
    [ ] the obligor is voluntarily underemployed.

ORDER OF CHILD SUPPORT
RCW 26.09.175; 26.26.132(5)
Page 2

WPF DR 01.0500 (8/91)

2 3.3 PERSON RECEIVING SUPPORT (OBLIGEE).

4   Name: Sue Snoopie
      Address: North 123 Beagle Street, Spokane Washington 99201
6
      Soc.Sec.Num: 456-11-1234
8   Employer: Acme Widget Co.

10   [x]   Monthly Net Income: $ 1,000
      [ ]   The income of the obligee is imputed at $ _____
12   because:

14   [ ]   the obligee's income is unknown.
            [ ]   the obligee is voluntarily unemployed.
16   [ ]   the obligee is voluntarily underemployed.

18   The parent receiving support may be required to submit an accounting of
      how the support is being spent to benefit the child.
20
   3.4 TRANSFER PAYMENT (check one of the boxes below).
22
      [x]   The obligor parent shall pay $ 213.00 _____ per month.
24   [ ]   The obligor parent shall pay the following amounts per month for the
            following children:
26
                        Name   Amount
28
30   _____ $ _____
      _____ $ _____
32   _____ $ _____
      _____ $ _____
34   _____ $ _____
      _____ $ _____
36   TOTAL MONTHLY AMOUNT $ _____

38
   3.5 STANDARD CALCULATION.
40
      $ 213.00 _____ per month. (See Worksheet A, line 15.)
42

ORDER OF CHILD SUPPORT
RCW 26.09.175; 26.26.132(5)
Page 3

119

WPF DR 01.0500 (8/91)

3.6   REASONS FOR DEVIATION FROM STANDARD CALCULATION.

[x]   The child support amount ordered in paragraph 3.4 does not deviate from the standard calculation.

[ ]   The child support amount ordered in paragraph 3.4 deviates from the standard calculation for the following reasons:

[ ]   Income of a new spouse;
[ ]   Income of other adults in the household;
[ ]   Child support actually received from other relationships;
[ ]   Gifts;
[ ]   Prizes;
[ ]   Possession of wealth;
[ ]   Extraordinary income of a child;
[ ]   Tax planning which results in greater benefit to the children;
[ ]   A nonrecurring source of income;
[ ]   Payment would reduce the parent's income level below the DSHS need standard;
[ ]   Extraordinary debt not voluntarily incurred;
[ ]   A significant disparity in the living costs of the parents due to conditions beyond their control;
[ ]   Special needs of disabled children;
[ ]   Special medical, educational, or psychological needs of the children;
[ ]   The child spends a significant amount of time with the parent who is obligated to make a support transfer payment;
[ ]   Children from other relationships;
[ ]   Other:

The factual basis for these reasons is as follows:

ORDER OF CHILD SUPPORT
RCW 26.09.175; 26.26.132(5)
Page 4

WPF DR 01.0500 (8/91)

2   3.7   REASONS WHY REQUEST FOR DEVIATION WAS DENIED.

4   [x]   Does not apply.

[ ]   The deviation sought by the [ ] obligor [ ] obligee was denied
6   because:

8   [ ]   no good reason exists to justify deviation.

        [ ]   other:

10

12

14

16

18

20

    3.8   STARTING DATE AND DAY TO BE PAID.
22

Starting Date: May 1, 1992
24   Day(s) of the month support is due: First day of each month.

26

28

30

32

34   [ ]   This is a modification of child support pursuant to RCW 26.09.170
        (8)(a) and (d) and the child support obligation set forth in Paragraph
36   3.4 shall be implemented in two equal increments as follows:

38

40

42

ORDER OF CHILD SUPPORT
RCW 26.09.175; 26.26.132(5)
Page 5

WPF DR 01.0500 (8/91)

2 3.9 HOW SUPPORT PAYMENTS SHALL BE MADE.

4   Support payments shall be made:

6   X [X]   to the Washington State Support Registry
             P.O. Box 9009
8   Olympia, WA 98507
             Phone: 1-800-922-4306

10

        [ ]   A notice of payroll deduction may be issued or other income
12   withholding action under Chapter 26.18 RCW or Chapter
               74.20A RCW may be taken, without further notice to the
14   obligor parent at any time after entry of an order by the court.
        [ ]   Wage withholding, by notice of payroll deduction or other
16   income withholding action under Chapter 26.18 RCW or
               Chapter 74.20A RCW, without further notice to the obligor,
18   is delayed until a payment is past due, because:

20   [ ]   there is good cause not to require immediate income
                      withholding.
22   [ ]   the parties have reached a written agreement which the
                      court approves that provides for an alternative
24   arrangement. (See below).

26   Each party shall notify the Washington State Support Registry of any
        change in residence address.
28
     [ ]   pursuant to the following alternative payment plan:
30

32

34   A notice of payroll deduction may issue or other income withholding
        action may be taken under RCW 26.18 or RCW 74.20A without prior
36   notice to the obligor:

38   [ ]   if a support payment is past due.
        [ ]   at any time.
40
        The order may be submitted to the Washington State Support
42   Registry for enforcement if a support payment is past due.

ORDER OF CHILD SUPPORT
RCW 26.09.175; 26.26.132(5)
Page 6

WPF DR 01.0500 (8/91)

2   3.10   TERMINATION OF SUPPORT.

4   Support shall be paid:

6   [ ]   until a permanent child support order is entered by this court.

       [ ]   until the child(ren) reach(es) the age of 18, except as otherwise

8   provided below in Paragraph 3.10.

      [X]   until the child(ren) reach(es) the age of 18 or completes high school,

10   whichever occurs last, except as otherwise provided below in

             Paragraph 3.10.

12   [ ]   after the age of 18 for _____

                                 (Name)

14   who is a dependnent adult child, until the child is capable of self-

          support and the necessity for support ceases.

16   [ ]   until the obligation for post secondary support set forth in Paragraph

             3.10 begins for the child(ren).

18   [ ]   other:

20

22

24

   3.11   POST SECONDARY EDUCATIONAL SUPPORT.

26

      [ ]   Does not apply.

28   [X]   The parents shall pay for the post secondary educational support of

          the child(ren) as follows:

30   The court reserves the rignt to enter an order as to

          post secondary education.

32

34

36

38

40

42

ORDER OF CHILD SUPPORT
RCW 26.09.175; 26.26.132(5)
Page 7

WPF DR 01.0500 (8/91)

2   3.12   DIRECT PAYMENT TO THIRD PARTIES FOR EXPENSES NOT
           INCLUDED IN THE TRANSFER PAYMENT.
4
           [x]   Does not apply.
6   [ ]   The mother shall pay _____ % and the father _____% of the
                 following expenses incurred on behalf of the children listed in
8   Paragraph 3.1:

10   [ ]   day care.
                 [ ]   educational expenses.
12   [ ]   long distance transportation expenses.
                 [ ]   other:
14
           [ ]   The obligor shall pay the following amounts each month the expense
16   is incurred on behalf of the children listed in Paragraph 3.1:

18   [ ]   day care: $ _____ to _____;
                 [ ]   educational expenses: $ _____ to _____;
20   [ ]   long distance transportation: $_____to _____
                       _____.
22   [ ]   other:

24   3.13   PERIODIC MODIFICATION.
26
           [ ]   Does not apply.
28   [x]   Child support shall be adjusted periodically as follows:
           Both parties are required to provide the other with income tax
30   returns for the preceeding two years on the first day of May of
           every even-numbered year for the purposeof recalculating support
           for the two years to follow.
32   3.14   INCOME TAX EXEMPTIONS.

34   [ ]   Does not apply.
           [ ]   Tax exemptions for the children shall be allocated as follows:
36   To the Petitioner

38

40
           [ ]   The parents shall sign the federal income tax dependency exemption
42   waiver.

ORDER OF CHILD SUPPORT
RCW 26.09.175; 26.26.132(5)
Page 8

WPF DR 01.0500 (8/91)

3.15   MEDICAL INSURANCE.

Health insurance coverage for the child(ren) listed in Paragraph 3.1 shall be provided by the [ ] mother [ ] father [x] both parents if coverage that can be extended to cover the child(ren) is or becomes available through employment or is union related and the cost of such coverage does not exceed $ _____(twenty-five percent of the obligated parent's basic child support obligation).

[x]   Health insurance coverage shall be provided as set forth above by the [ ] mother [ ] father [x] both parents, even if the cost of such coverage exceeds 25% of the obligated parent's basic child support obligation.

[ ]   The reasons for not ordering the [ ] mother [ ] father to provide health insurance coverage for the child(ren) are:

The parents shall maintain health insurance coverage, as set forth in paragraph 3.1, if available, until further order of the court or until health insurance is no longer available through the parents' employer or union and no conversion privileges exist to continue coverage following termination of employment.

A parent who is required under this order to provide health insurance coverage is liable for any covered health care costs for which that parent receives direct payment from an insurer.

A parent who is required under this order to provide health insurance coverage shall provide proof of such coverage within twenty days of the entry of this order or within twenty days of the date such coverage becomes available, to:

[x]   the physical custodian.
[ ]   the Washington State Support Registry if the parent has been notified or ordered to make payments to the Washington State Support Registry.

If proof of health insurance coverage is not provided within twenty days the obligee or the Department of Social and Health Services may seek direct enforcement of the coverage through the obligor's employer or union without further notice to the obligor as provided under Chapter 26.18 RCW.

ORDER OF CHILD SUPPORT
RCW 26.09.175; 26.26.132(5)
Page 9

SAMPLE #17 — Continued

WPF DR 01.0500 (8/91)

2 3.16 EXTRAORDINARY HEALTH CARE EXPENSES.

4 ^{OB} The OBLIGOR shall pay __50__% of extraordinary health care expenses
(the obligor's proportional share of income from the Support Schedule
6 Worksheet A, line 6), if monthly medical expenses exceed $ __45__ per
child (5% of the basic support obligation from Worksheet A, line 5).

8

3.17 BACK CHILD SUPPORT.

10
X [x] Does not apply.
12 [ ] The obligee parent is awarded a judgment against the obligor parent
in the amount of $ _____ for back child support for
14 the period from _____ to _____.
            (Date)   (Date)

16

3.18 OTHER.

18

20

22

24

26
Dated: _____April 12, 199-_____   *J. M Commissioner*
28   Judge/Commissioner

30 Presented by: Approved for entry:
                                            Notice of presentation waived:
32

34 *Sue Snoopie*   _____
Signature and Washington State Bar   Signature and Washington State Bar
36 Number, if applicable   Number, if applicable
Sue Snoopie, Petitioner
38 I apply for full support enforcement services.

40 *Sue Snoopie*
Signature of Party
42

ORDER OF CHILD SUPPORT
RCW 26.09.175; 26.26.132(5)
Page 10

126

WPF DR 03.0300 (7/91)

SUPERIOR COURT OF WASHINGTON
COUNTY OF SPOKANE

In re the Marriage of:

SUE SNOOPIE,   Petitioner
and
SAM SNOOPIE,   Respondent.

NO.

NOTE FOR DISSOLUTION CALENDAR (NON-CONTESTED CASE--OPTIONAL)

TO THE CLERK OF COURT AND TO: SAM SNOOPIE

1.   Please note that this case will be placed on the non-contested dissolution calendar for hearing on the date set out below.

2.   A hearing has been set for the following date, time and place.

Date: April 12, 199-

Time: 9:30   a.m./p.m.-

Place: Spokane County Court House

Room/Department: Room 300

Dated: ___March 20, 199-___

Sue Snoopie
Signature of Lawyer or Party
(if party has no lawyer)

Sue Snoopie
Typed Name and Washington State
Bar Number, if applicable

NOTE FOR DISSOLUTION CALENDAR
CR 40
Page 1

IN THE SUPERIOR COURT OF THE STATE OF WASHINGTON
COUNTY OF Spokane

In Re the Marriage of:

No. 8800000

Sue Snoopie }
PETITIONER }

Declaration of
Non-Military Service

- and -

Sam Snoopie }
RESPONDENT }

STATE OF WASHINGTON }
}   ss.
COUNTY OF Spokane }

Sue Snoopie , declares under penalty of perjury under the laws of the state of Washington that the following is true:

I am the Petitioner, above named. I am the spouse of Sam Snoopie who is the Respondent, above named. I know of my own personal knowledge that the Respondent is not in the military service of the United States. This declaration is made in connection with the entry of a Decree of Dissolution in the above entitled proceeding and is made pursuant to the provisions of the Soldiers and Sailors' Civil Relief Act of March 4, 1918, as amended.

Sue Snoopie
Petitioner

WAIVER OF RIGHTS UNDER SOLDIERS AND SAILORS'
CIVIL RELIEF ACT AND ADMISSION OF SERVICE

IN THE SUPERIOR COURT OF THE STATE OF WASHINGTON
COUNTY OF Spokane

In Re the Marriage of:

No. 8800000

Sue Snoopie
       PETITIONER

- and -

Sam Snoopie
      RESPONDENT

Waiver of Rights Under
Soldiers and Sailors'
Civil Relief Act and
Admission of Service

My name is Sam Snoopie and I am the above named Respondent. My spouse has petitioned the above-entitled court to terminate our marriage under the laws of the state of Washington. I am a member of the United States military service and I am informed of my rights under the Soldiers and Sailors' Civil Relief Act of March 4, 1918, as amended. I do hereby waive my rights under the Soldiers and Sailors' Civil Relief Act and I request the court to terminate our marriage as requested by the Petitioner.

I received a copy of the Summons and Petition in this matter as issued by the court under the above case number on the 3rd day of March , 199- .

I admit and acknowledge service of process upon me in this matter.

Sam Snoopie
(signature)

Name: Sam Snoopie

Rank: Corporal

Serial Number: 98765-432

Unit: 007

Subscribed and sworn to before me this 10th day of March , 199-

I. M. Judge
Judge Advocate

5

MISCELLANEOUS MATTERS

a. IF YOUR SPOUSE IS MISSING, OR YOU CANNOT AFFORD A PROCESS SERVER, OR YOUR SPOUSE IS OUT OF STATE

1. Service by publication

If you do not know where your spouse is, you may be able to serve him or her by publication. In order to do that you have to get a judge's signature on an order. The forms for publishing are:

(a) Form DR 01.0260, Declaration for Service of Summons by Publication, (see Sample #21),

(b) Form DR 01.0265, Order for Service of Summons by Publication, (see Sample #22), and

(c) Form DR 01.0270, Summons by Publication, (see Sample #23.) (This form must be published in a newspaper).

Be warned: you will not be able to get what is called "personal relief" by this process. That is, you will not be awarded any property, child support, or maintenance; only the dissolution of your marriage and custody of the children are settled by this process.

2. Service by mail

Service by mail is an alternative in the following circumstances:

(a) Your spouse lives out of state,

(b) Your spouse has consistently avoided personal service,

(c) You have no friend or relative who could serve your spouse, or

(d) You don't have the money for an out-of-state server.

Samples #24, #25, and #26 show how you would prepare the forms in this case.

b. IF YOU HAVE WAITED MORE THAN A YEAR BETWEEN DATE OF PETITION AND PROCEEDING WITH YOUR DIVORCE

If more than a year has elapsed between your filing of the Petition and the continuation of your divorce, you will have to show the court that you have given your spouse notice of your intention to proceed.

If you served your spouse the Petition with a Summons, and he or she did not respond, you must send a copy of the Notice of Taking Default and Entry of Decree of Dissolution After One Year (see Sample #27). The original Notice of Taking Default and Entry of Decree of Dissolution After One Year should be given to the county clerk, who will place it in your file. When you receive the return receipt with your spouse's signature from the post office, attach it to the Declaration of Mailing (see Sample #28).

You must take the Declaration of Mailing with you when you go to court for your Decree of Dissolution as proof of notice to your spouse of the re-commencement of the divorce proceedings.

c. HOW TO DISCONTINUE YOUR DIVORCE

If you have reconciled with your spouse or if you decide for any reason that you cannot go through with the divorce, there are two ways to stop the court proceedings:

(a) If you do nothing more, the county clerk will dismiss the action after a year.

(b) You may fill out a Motion for Non-Suit and Order of Dismissal (see

Sample #29) and take it to the courthouse. Ask the county clerk for your file and take your file to the presiding judge or commissioner. Present the judge or commissioner with the Motion for Non-Suit and Order for Dismissal and explain that you want to discontinue your divorce. The judge will sign the form and your case will be dismissed. Return the divorce file to the county clerk.

Once your case has been dismissed, if you should ever wish to begin divorce proceedings again, you will have to begin from the beginning by filing a new Petition and paying the filing fee. The county clerk will open a new court file and give you a new number.

d. HOW TO APPLY FOR FINANCIAL AID

As stated earlier in this book, when you begin your divorce proceedings by filing your Petition for Dissolution of the Marriage and your Summons (required if you and your spouse are not filing jointly), you must pay a filing fee to the county clerk.

If paying this fee would be a financial hardship to you, you may apply to the court to have this fee waived. If your spouse lives outside Washington, the court may also allow you to serve your spouse by certified mail rather than having the expense of service by sheriff.

The procedure by which you ask for this financial consideration is called In Forma Pauperis. First you fill out your Petition and Summons as outlined previously in this book. Then you fill out a Motion and Declaration for Order to Commence and Prosecute Proceeding In Forma Pauperis (see Sample #30). You also fill out an Order Authorizing Proceeding In Forma Pauperis (see Sample #31).

Next, take these forms to the courthouse and ask the county clerk which judge or court commissioner is authorized to sign your Order and Motion for Proceeding In Forma Pauperis. Then go to that judge or court commissioner's courtroom and ask for the bailiff. Show the bailiff your papers: the Order Authorizing Proceedings In Forma Pauperis should be on top, the Motion and Declaration for Order to Commence and Prosecute Proceeding In Forma Pauperis should be next, and the Summons and Petition should be third and fourth.

The bailiff will take you before the judge or court commissioner and will hand your forms to him or her. You should then give the court commissioner the following information:

(a) Your name and address, as well as your spouse's

(b) The fact that you intend to terminate the marriage because it is irretrievably broken

(c) The fact that you do not have the funds to pay the filing fees or the notary fees for your Petition

(d) Ask the court to sign your motion to proceed In Forma Pauperis

You may wish to write this information out in a politely worded paragraph and read it to the judge or court commissioner. He or she will then ask you some questions about your financial situation. If your funds are limited and barely meet your living costs, the court may decide that you cannot afford the court costs.

After the judge signs your Motion and Order In Forma Pauperis, take all your papers to the county clerk. He or she will stamp them "filed," and give you your case number.

If your spouse lives outside Washington, and you know the address, ask the court for permission to serve the Summons and Petition by certified mail rather than through a sheriff or process server in another state. This will save you cost of service.

When you receive the return receipt with your spouse's signature from the post office, fill out the Declaration of Mailing (see Sample #32) and attach the return receipt to it. Sign the Declaration of Mailing and take it to the county clerk for filing.

SAMPLE #21
DECLARATION FOR SERVICE OF SUMMONS
BY PUBLICATION (DR 01.0260)

WPF DR 01.0260 (7/91)

SUPERIOR COURT OF WASHINGTON
COUNTY OF SPOKANE

In re the Marriage of:

SUE SNOOPIE,   Petitioner

and

SAM SNOOPIE,   Respondent.

NO.

DECLARATION FOR SERVICE
OF SUMMONS BY
PUBLICATION
(DCLR)

I DECLARE:

1.   The summons in this matter needs to be served on the respondent by publication because:

      [x]   the respondent is not a resident of this state.
      [ ]   the respondent cannot be found in this state because:

2.   The following efforts were made to locate the respondent for personal service or service by mail: I have made careful inquiry of relations, friends, and business associates of the Respondent and I cannot learn of his present wherabouts. I know of no address to which I could mail the Summons to the Respondent. The following are the names of persons that I have contacted: Emily Snoopie, John Jackson, Bob Sneaky.

3.   [ ]   A copy of the summons (substantially in the form prescribed in RCW 4.28.110) and the petition have been deposited in the post office, directed to the respondent at the respondent's place of residence.
      [x]   I do not know the respondent's address.

I declare under penalty of perjury under the laws of the State of Washington that the foregoing is true and correct.

Signed at ___Spokane, Washington_____, on __3/30/9-___.
                    (City and State)   (Date)

                                        _Sue Snoopie_____
                                              Signature
                                        Sue Snoopie
                                        _____
                                          Typed Name

DECLARATION FOR SERVICE BY PUBLICATION
RCW 4.28.100
Page 1

SAMPLE #22
ORDER FOR SERVICE OF SUMMONS
BY PUBLICATION (DR 01.0265)

WPF DR 01.0265 (7/91)

SUPERIOR COURT OF WASHINGTON
COUNTY OF SPOKANE

In re the Marriage of:

SUE SNOOPIE,   Petitioner

and

SAM SNOOPIE,   Respondent.

NO. 92000
ORDER FOR SERVICE OF
SUMMONS BY PUBLICATION
(If Required By Local
Practice)
(ORPUB)

I. BASIS

The court has considered a declaration stating that the summons in this matter needs to be served on the respondent by publication.

II. FINDINGS

Based on the representations made in the declaration, the court FINDS that the summons in this matter should be served on the respondent by publication in accordance with RCW 4.28.100.

III. ORDER

IT IS ORDERED that the summons in this matter be served on the respondent by publication in conformity with RCW 4.28.100.

Dated: March 30, 199- _____   _J. M. Commissioner_
                                                Judge/Commissioner

Presented by:

Sue Snoopie
Signature and Washington State Bar
Number, if applicable
Sue Snoopie

ORDER ALLOWING SERVICE BY PUBLICATION
RCW 4.28.100
Page 1

SAMPLE #23
SUMMONS BY PUBLICATION (DR 01.0270)

WPF DR 01.0270 (7/91)

SUPERIOR COURT OF WASHINGTON
COUNTY OF SPOKANE

In re the Marriage of:

SUE SNOOPIE,   Petitioner

and

SAM SNOOPIE,   Respondent.

NO. 92000

SUMMONS BY PUBLICATION
(SMPB)

TO THE RESPONDENT:

1. The petitioner has started an action in the above court requesting:

    [x] that your marriage be dissolved.
    [ ] a legal separation.
    [ ] that your marriage be declared invalid.

2. The petition also requests that the Court grant the following relief:

    [ ] Provide reasonable maintenance for the [ ] husband [ ] wife.
    [x] Approve a parenting plan for the dependent children.
    [x] Determine support for the dependent children pursuant to the Washington State Support Schedule.
    [ ] Approve a separation agreement;
    [ ] Dispose of property and liabilities.
    [x] Change name of wife to: __Sue Smith_____.
    [ ] Change name of husband to: _____.
    [ ] Order payment of court costs and reasonable fees.
    [ ] Enter a permanent restraining order.
    [ ] Order payment of day care expenses for the children.
    [ ] Award the tax exemptions for the dependent children as follows:

    [ ] Order payment of attorney's fees, other professional fees and costs.
    [ ] Other:

SUMMONS BY PUBLICATION
RCW 4.28.100; CR 4.1
Page 1

134

SAMPLE #23 — Continued

WPF DR 01.0270 (7/91)

3. You must respond to this summons by serving a copy of your written response on the person signing this summons and by filing the original with the clerk of the court. If you do not serve your written response within 60 days after the date of the first publication of this summons (60 days after the ___30th___ day of ___March___, 199___), the court may enter an order of default against you, and at the end of 90 days after service and filing, the court may, without further notice to you, enter a decree and approve or provide for other relief requested in this summons. If you serve a notice of appearance on the undersigned person, you are entitled to notice before an order of default or a decree may be entered.

4. Your written response to the summons must be on forms approved by the Office of the Administrator for the Courts. These forms may be obtained by contacting the clerk of the court or the Office of the Administrator for the Courts at:

>   Office of the Administrator for the Courts
>   Temple of Justice, AV-01
>   Olympia, Washington 98504
>   (206) 357-2129

5. If this action has not been filed with the court, you may demand that the petitioner file this action with the court. If you do so, the demand must be in writing and must be served upon the person publishing this summons. Within 14 days after you serve the demand, the petitioner must file this action with the court, or the service on you of this summons will be void.

6. If you wish to seek the advice of an attorney in this matter, you should do so promptly so that your written response, if any, may be served on time.

7. One method of serving a copy of your response on the petitioner is to send it by certified mail with return receipt requested.

8. Other:

SUMMONS BY PUBLICATION
RCW 4.28.100; CR 4.1
Page 2

WPF DR 01.0270 (7/91)

2   This summons is issued pursuant to RCW 4.28.100 and Superior Court Civil Rule 4.1 of the State of Washington.

4   Dated: March 30, 199-
_____

Sue Snoopie

6   Signature of Lawyer or Petitioner (if petitioner has no lawyer)

8

Sue Snoopie
_____

10   Print or Type Name (include Washington State Bar Number, if applicable)

12

14   FILE ORIGINAL WITH THE CLERK OF THE COURT AT: SERVE A COPY OF YOUR RESPONSE ON:

16

18   [x] Petitioner
[ ] Petitioner's Lawyer

20   Spokane Superior Court
_____   Sue Snoopie
_____

(Name of Court)   (Name)

22   North 123 Beagle Street

24   _____
(Address)   (Address)

26   _____   Spokane, WA 99201
_____

28

30   Phone: _____

32

34

36

38

40

42

SUMMONS BY PUBLICATION
RCW 4.28.100; CR 4.1
Page 3

SAMPLE #24
REQUEST FOR ORDER TO SERVE SUMMONS
AND PETITION BY MAIL (DR 01.0280)

WPF DR 01.0280 (7/91)

SUPERIOR COURT OF WASHINGTON
COUNTY OF SPOKANE

In re the Marriage of:

SUE SNOOPIE,   Petitioner
and
SAM SNOOPIE,   Respondent.

NO.   92000

REQUEST FOR ORDER TO
SERVE SUMMONS AND
PETITION BY MAIL
(RQ)

1.   I request that the court issue an order allowing the summons and petition in this matter to be served on the respondent by mail.

2.   I believe that service should be made by mail because:

[ ]   the respondent is not a resident of this state.
[ ]   the respondent cannot be found in this state.
[x]   I am indigent and cannot afford service by publication.

3.   I have not been able to locate or serve the respondent, even through the respondent's employer, friends or family.

4.   Service by mail is just as likely to provide actual notice as service by publication.

5.   The mailings should be sent to the following address:

6000 East 6000 - 14th Ave., Yakima, WA 98083

REQUEST FOR ORDER TO SERVE BY MAIL
RCW 4.28.100; CR 4(d)(4)
Page 1

WPF DR 01.0280 (7/91)

2   6.   This address is:

4   [X]   The last known address of the respondent.
         [ ]   The respondent's parent or nearest living relative.
6   [ ]   Other:

8

10

12   Dated: _March 30, 199-_____   *Sue Snoopie*
                                   Signature of Lawyer or Petitioner (if
14   petitioner has no lawyer)

16

                                     Sue Snoopie
18   Print or Type Name (include Washington
                                     State Bar Number, if applicable)
20

I declare under penalty of perjury under the laws of the State of Washington that
22 the foregoing is true and correct.

24   Signed at _Spokane, Washington_____, on _3/30/9-____.
                     (City and State)   (Date)
26
                               Sue Snoopie
28   Signature

30   Sue Snoopie
                                   Print or Type Name

32

34

36

38

40

42

REQUEST FOR ORDER TO SERVE BY MAIL
RCW 4.28.100; CR 4(d)(4)
Page 2

SAMPLE #25
ORDER ALLOWING SERVICE OF SUMMONS
AND PETITION BY MAIL (DR 01.0285)

WPF DR 01.0285 (7/91)

SUPERIOR COURT OF WASHINGTON
COUNTY OF SPOKANE

In re the Marriage of:

SUE SNOOPIE,

                    Petitioner

and

SAM SNOOPIE,

                    Respondent.

NO. 92000

ORDER ALLOWING SERVICE OF SUMMONS AND PETITION BY MAIL
(ORRSR)

I. BASIS

The court has considered an affidavit requesting an order allowing the summons and petition in this matter to be served on the respondent by mail.

II. FINDINGS

Based on the case record to date and the representations made in the affidavit, the court FINDS that the summons and petition in this matter should be served on the respondent by mail in accordance with CR 4(d)(4).

III. ORDER

IT IS ORDERED:

3.1   The summons and petition in this matter be served on the respondent by mail by a person 18 years of age or over and competent to be a witness <u>but not the petitioner.</u>

3.2   Two (2) copies shall be mailed postage prepaid, one by ordinary first class mail, and the other by certified mail, return receipt requested, showing when, and to whom, delivered, each showing a return address for the sender or an address through which correspondence may be directed to the sender.

3.3   The mailings shall be sent to the following address:

    East 6000 - 14th Ave., Yakima, WA 98093

ORDER ALLOWING SERVICE BY MAIL
CR 4(d)
Page 1

WPF DR 01.0285 (7/91)

2   3.4   This address is:

4   [X]   The last known address of the respondent.
         [ ]   The respondent's parent or nearest living relative.
6   [ ]   Other:

8
     3.5   A summons and petition mailed to the respondent care of parents or other
10   individuals shall be addressed directly to the parent or other individual with
            a note enclosed asking that the summons and petition be delivered to the
12   respondent.

14   3.6   The person mailing the summons and petition shall complete a Return of
            Service form approved by the Office of the Administrator for the Courts.
16

18   .
     Dated: _March 30, 199-_____   *I. M. Commissioner*
20   Judge/Commissioner

22
     Presented by:
24
     Sue Snoopie
26   Signature and Washington State Bar
     Number, if applicable
28
     Sue Snoopie, Petitioner
30

32

34

36

38

40

42

ORDER ALLOWING SERVICE BY MAIL
CR 4(d)
Page 2

WPF DR 01.0290 (7/91)

SUPERIOR COURT OF WASHINGTON
COUNTY OF SPOKANE

In re the Marriage of:

NO. 92000

SUE SNOOPIE,   Petitioner
and

SUMMONS BY MAIL
(SM)

SAM SNOOPIE,   Respondent.

TO THE RESPONDENT:

1.   The petitioner has started an action in the above court requesting:

    [X]   that your marriage be dissolved.
    [ ]   a legal separation.
    [ ]   that your marriage be declared invalid.

    Additional requests, if any, are stated in the petition, a copy of which is attached.

2.   You must respond to this summons by serving a copy of your written response on the person signing this summons and by filing the original with the clerk of the court. If you do not serve your written response within 90 days from the date of mailing of this summons (90 days after the _30th_ day of _March_, 199_), the court may enter an order of default against you, and at the end of 90 days after service and filing, the court may, without further notice to you, enter a decree and approve or provide for other relief requested in this summons. If you serve a notice of appearance on the undersigned person, you are entitled to notice before an order of default or a decree may be entered.

3.   Your written response to the summons and petition must be on forms approved by the Office of the Administrator for the Courts. These forms may be obtained by contacting the clerk of the court or the Office of the Administrator for the Courts at:

        Office of the Administrator for the Courts
        Temple of Justice, AV-01
        Olympia, Washington 98504
        (206) 357-2129

SUMMONS BY MAIL
RCW 4.28.100; CR 4(d)(4); CR 4.1
Page 1

SAMPLE #26 — Continued

WPF DR 01.0290 (7/91)

4. If this action has not been filed with the court, you may demand that the petitioner file this action with the court. If you do so, the demand must be in writing and must be served upon the person publishing this summons. Within 14 days after you serve the demand, the petitioner must file this action with the court, or the service on you of this summons will be void.

5. If you wish to seek the advice of an attorney in this matter, you should do so promptly so that your written response, if any, may be served on time.

6. One method of serving a copy of your response on the petitioner is to send it by certified mail with return receipt requested.

This summons is issued pursuant to RCW 4.28.100 and Superior Court Civil Rule 4.1 of the State of Washington.

Dated: March 30, 199-

Sue Snoopie

Signature of Lawyer or Petitioner (if petitioner has no lawyer)

Sue Snoopie

Print or Type Name (include Washington State Bar Number, if applicable)

FILE ORIGINAL WITH THE CLERK OF THE COURT AT:

SERVE A COPY OF YOUR RESPONSE ON:

[x] Petitioner
[ ] Petitioner's Lawyer

Spokane Superior Court

(Name of Court)

Sue Snoopie

(Name)

North 123 Beagle Street

(Address)

(Address)

Spokane, WA 99201

Phone: _____

Date Mailed: March 30, 199-

SUMMONS BY MAIL
RCW 4.28.100; CR 4(d)(4); CR 4.1
Page 2

NOTICE OF TAKING DEFAULT AND
ENTRY OF DECREE OF DISSOLUTION AFTER ONE YEAR

IN THE SUPERIOR COURT OF THE STATE OF WASHINGTON
COUNTY OF Spokane

In re the Marriage of:

No. 8800000

Sue Snoopie
          PETITIONER }

- and -

Sam Snoopie
          RESPONDENT }

**Notice of Taking Default
and Entry of Decree of
Dissolution After One Year**

TO: Sam Snoopie   , Respondent, above named.

YOU ARE HEREBY NOTIFIED that more than ten (10) days from the date you receive this notice, on the 24th day of January, 199-,* by certified mail or in person, I will present to the Superior Court of the state of Washington in and for the County of Spokane, an Order of Default, Conclusions of Law, Findings of Fact and Decree of Dissolution (divorce) for entry by said court. Said proposed Decree that I will present for entry will follow the request of the Petition herein.

This notice is in compliance with Rule 55f(1)(B) for the Superior Court of the state of Washington. This notice is sent to you by certified mail, return receipt requested, and the return receipt has been filed with the clerk of the court.

Done this 10th day of January, 199 - .

IN PERSON

Sue Snoopie
(signature of petitioner)

*This date must be at least 13 days after the day you mail it.

SAMPLE #28
DECLARATION OF MAILING

IN THE SUPERIOR COURT OF THE STATE OF WASHINGTON
COUNTY OF Spokane

In re the Marriage of:

No. 8800000

Sue Snoopie
   PETITIONER

- and -

Sam Snoopie
   RESPONDENT

**Declaration of Mailing
(Notice of Taking Default
and Entry of Decree of Dissolution)**

STATE OF WASHINGTON }
         } ss.
COUNTY OF Spokane   }

The undersigned declares under penalty of perjury under the laws of the state of Washington that the following is true: ~~he~~ (she) is the petitioner, herein. That ~~he~~ (she) placed in the United States mails an envelope(s) with a certified mail receipt attached; together with correct postage affixed, addressed to the respondent at the following last known address~~(es)~~:

Sam Snoopie East 600000 - 14th Avenue Yakima, Washington 98093

Said envelope(s) contained a certified copy of the Notice of Taking Default and Entry of Decree of Dissolution, when more than one year has elapsed after the start of this proceeding.

☒ A return receipt was received back from the Post Office Department bearing the signature of the respondent. Said receipt is attached to this declaration in support of the taking of default and entry of Decree of Dissolution, herein.

☐ The mailed envelope(s) was (were) returned by the Post Office Department indicating that the Post Office Department was unable to deliver the envelope(s) to the respondent. The petitioner has also given Notice of Taking Default and Entry of Decree Dissolution by one publication in a newspaper of general circulation in this county. A copy of the newspaper's affidavit concerning said publication is attached hereto.

Snoopie

(petitioner's signature)

MOTION FOR NON-SUIT AND ORDER OF DISMISSAL

IN THE SUPERIOR COURT OF THE STATE OF WASHINGTON
COUNTY OF <u>Spokane</u>

In re the Marriage of:

No. <u>8800000</u>

<u>Sue Snoopie</u>
     PETITIONER }

- and -

<u>Sam Snoopie</u>
     RESPONDENT }

**Motion for Non-Suit and
Order of Dismissal**

MOTION

Comes now the Petitioner, above-named, stating that he (she) no longer wishes to terminate their marriage and, therefore, moves for Non-Suit and Order of Dismissal.

Sam Snoopie
Respondent — In Person

Sue Snoopie
Petitioner — In Person

ORDER

Upon presentation of the above Motion for Non-Suit and Order of Dismissal, the court having examined the court file in this matter and being fully advised in the premises, it is by the court ORDERED, that said motion be and the same is hereby granted. THIS CASE IS DISMISSED.

Done in open Court this <u>5th</u> day of <u>January</u>, 19<u>9-</u>.

J. M. Commissioner
Judge/Court Commissioner

Presented by:

Sue Snoopie
Petitioner — In Person

SAMPLE #30
MOTION AND DECLARATION FOR ORDER TO COMMENCE AND PROSECUTE PROCEEDING IN FORMA PAUPERIS

IN THE SUPERIOR COURT OF THE STATE OF WASHINGTON,
COUNTY OF <u>Spokane</u>

In re the Marriage of:

No. <u>8800000</u>

<u>Sue Snoopie</u>
    PETITIONER

- and -

<u>Sam Snoopie</u>
    RESPONDENT

Motion and Declaration for Order to Commence and Prosecute Proceeding In Forma Pauperis

STATE OF WASHINGTON

COUNTY OF <u>Spokane</u>

ss.

<u>Sue Snoopie</u>   ,declares under penalty of perjury under the laws of the state of Washington that the following is true:

I.
I am one of the parties in the above-entitled proceeding. My marriage to <u>Sam Snoopie</u> is irretrievably broken. We are at this time unable to live together as married persons. This proceeding to terminate our marriage is brought in good faith and it is my present intention to proceed to a final dissolution of our marriage.

II.
I bring this proceeding in person, without an attorney, because I lack financial means to pay legal counsel. I cannot, without financial hardship, pay to the clerk of this court the statutory fee for filing my Petition.

WHEREFORE, I request the court for:

(1) ☒ An order allowing commencement and prosecution of this proceeding In Forma Pauperis;

(2) ☒ An order directing the clerk of this court to file and issue my Petition or any other papers herein without any fee, cost or charge whatsoever;

(3) ☒ An order of this court authorizing me to serve the Summons and Petition upon my spouse by certified mail without return receipt, deposited with the court at the time of the final hearing herein.

Sue Snoopie
_____
(petitioner's signature)

IN THE SUPERIOR COURT OF THE STATE OF WASHINGTON
COUNTY OF <u>Spokane</u>

In re the Marriage of:

No. <u>8800000</u>

<u>Sue Snoopie</u>
　　　　　　　　PETITIONER 　}
　　　　　　　　　　　　　　}　　　**Order Authorizing Proceeding**
- and -　　　　　　　　　　 }　　　**In Forma Pauperis**
　　　　　　　　　　　　　　}
<u>Sam Snoopie</u>　　　　　　}
　　　　　　　　RESPONDENT }

The Petitioner, above named, having presented to the court a sufficient affidavit and declaration to proceed In Forma Pauperis and the court being of the opinion that the order asked for should issue, now therefore, it is:

　☒　ORDERED, ADJUDGED, and DECREED that the parties are hereby authorized to prosecute this action In Forma Pauperis; and the clerk of this court is ordered and directed to file and issue papers and pleadings as requested by either party without prepayment of any fee, cost or charge whatsoever. In approving this order, the court reserves the right to review this authorization and require the payment of the fee if justified at the time of final hearing.

　☒　It is further ORDERED, ADJUDGED, and DECREED that the Petitioner, herein, is authorized to serve the Summons and Petition, herein, on the Respondent by certified mail with the post office return receipt deposited with the court at the time of the final hearing herein.

Done in open Court this <u>5th</u> day of <u>January</u> , 199 <u>-</u> .

　　　　　　　　　　　　　　　　　I. M. Commissioner
　　　　　　　　　　　　　　　　　Judge/Court Commissioner

Presented by:
Sue Snoopie
In Person

149

IN THE SUPERIOR COURT OF THE STATE OF WASHINGTON
COUNTY OF <u>Spokane</u>

In re the Marriage of:

No. <u>8800000</u>

<u>Sue Snoopie</u>
        PETITIONER }

- and -

<u>Sam Snoopie</u>
        RESPONDENT }

Declaration of Mailing

STATE OF WASHINGTON   }
                    } ss.
COUNTY OF <u>Spokane</u>   }

The undersigned declares under penalty of perjury under the laws of the state of Washington that the following is true: ~~he~~ (she) is the petitioner, herein. That ~~he~~ (she) placed in the United States mails an envelope(~~s~~) with a certified mail receipt attached; together with correct postage affixed, addressed to the respondent at the following last known address(~~es~~):

<u>Sam Snoopie East 600000 - 14th Avenue Yakima, Washington 98093</u>

Said envelope(s) contained a copy of each of the following documents:

<u>Summons Petition</u>

☒ A return receipt was received back from the Post Office Department bearing the signature of the respondent. Said receipt is attached to this declaration in support of the taking of default and entry of Decree of Dissolution, herein.

Sue Snoopie
(petitioner's signature)

GLOSSARY

ACKNOWLEDGE
The signature and seal of a notary public

ACTION
The suit for dissolution of marriage that a person brings to end his or her marriage

ADVERTISING
In this context, a legal notice published in a newspaper

AFFIDAVIT
A written statement signed in front of a notary public and witnessed by the notary

AMEND
The addition of words to a paper that is filed with the county clerk concerning a dissolution of marriage

ANNULMENT
The termination of an illegal marriage, called "declaration of invalidity" in Washington's divorce act

APPEAL
To ask a higher court to decide if the dissolution is proper and legal

APPEARANCE
The filing of a paper with the county clerk contesting the dissolution and refusing the requests of the petitioner

BAILIFF
The judge's assistant in court

BENCH
The judge or court commissioner's seat in the courtroom

CASE NUMBER
A number that is placed on the Petition when it is filed. The same number is used on all other papers filed in the same action.

CERTIFIED COPY
A copy of something that the county clerk places a seal on and states that the copy is the same as the original in the court file

CONTEMPT OF COURT
The failure to do something the court has ordered

CONTESTED DIVORCE
When the respondent does not agree with the claims and requests of the Petition and files a paper with the county clerk stating his or her objections

COOPERATIVE
When both spouses want the divorce and agree with the requests in the Petition

COUNTY ASSESSOR
An elected public official at the county courthouse who will provide the legal description of real estate if given the street address

COUNTY CLERK
An elected public official who keeps the court records and with whom dissolution papers are filed at the county courthouse

COURT COMMISSIONER
A person appointed by the court to sign dissolution papers on behalf of a judge

DECISION
The ruling of the judge or court commissioner when the spouses do not agree

DECREE OF DISSOLUTION
The paper that dissolves a marriage when signed by a judge or court commissioner

DECREE OF SEPARATE MAINTENANCE
A paper signed by the judge or court commissioner that keeps a couple married, but living separate and apart

DEED
A legal paper transferring ownership of real estate from seller to buyer

DEFAULT
When the respondent fails to file a paper objecting to what was asked for in the Petition for Dissolution

DEFAULT DIVORCE CALENDAR
A list of the divorce cases to be heard by the judge or court commissioner on a certain day, also called a "Default Divorce Docket"

ENCUMBRANCE
The unpaid balance due on a house or any other property

EQUITY
The duty a judge or court commissioner has to be fair to both parties; also the value of a house or other property less balance due on the purchase price

FEES
Payment to the county clerk for filing a Petition; also the wages paid to an attorney, a sheriff, or a process server

"FILED" STAMP
The stamp the county clerk uses on copies of papers submitted to show the date they are filed with the county clerk

HARASSMENT
Annoying or threatening to harm someone or his or her children or property

INDIGENT
Having money for living expenses only with nothing left over

IN FORMA PAUPERIS
A legal term for asking the court to waive your filing fees

JUDGMENT
The decision of the judge or court commission; it is a part of the Decree of Dissolution

LEGAL DESCRIPTION
The description of the location of real estate which differs from the street address

LEGAL NOTICES
Publication in a weekly newspaper in the classified ad section, giving notice of a court proceeding

LEGAL SERVICES OFFICE
An attorney's office that gives free legal help to eligible clients

LITIGANT
A person in a lawsuit; a petitioner is a litigant

MAINTENANCE
The money paid by one spouse to another after the divorce; formerly called "alimony"

MODIFY
To change the custody or support of a child after the Decree of Dissolution has been signed by the judge or court commissioner

MOTION
A request to the court asking that something be done, such as issuing a Restraining Order

NONSUPPORT
The failure of a person to support his or her family

NOTARY PUBLIC
Someone appointed by the governor of the state of Washington, before whom you sign your papers, if required; notaries work at banks, real estate offices, and insurance companies

OATH
To make a statement in which one promises to tell the truth to the judge or court commissioner

PETITION
The paper requesting a dissolution of marriage; it is filed at the county clerk's office

PETITIONER
The person asking the court for a dissolution of marriage

PLEADING
Any paper in the court file concerning a dissolution

PROCESS
The delivery of papers to the appropriate person and the sworn statement of the person who delivered the papers that they have been delivered

PROCESS SERVER

The person who delivers papers and makes a sworn statement that they were delivered properly

PROPERTY SETTLEMENT AGREEMENT

A written contract between two spouses agreeing to a division of property and debts, and custody and support of the children

PUBLISH

Placement of a legal notice in a weekly newspaper

R.C.W.

Revised Code of Washington; Washington state laws

RECONCILED

To resume living together as husband and wife

RECONCILIATION PERIOD

The 90-day waiting period from the time that the Petition is given to the county clerk and a copy of the Petition is sent to the respondent spouse to the time the judge or court commissioner grants the dissolution

RESPONDENT

The spouse who is not filing the Petition of Dissolution

RESTRAINING ORDER

A paper signed by a judge or court commissioner that prohibits a person from doing something or orders a person to do something

APPENDIX
A CHECKLIST OF STEPS TO TAKE

These lists summarize the steps that will need to be followed whether you obtain your own divorce or have an attorney handle your case. This summary can serve as a checklist. Be sure that you understand the details of each of the procedures as explained in this book.

a.   IF YOU AND YOUR SPOUSE BOTH SIGN THE PETITION

1.   Fill out the Petition and sign.

2.   Have your spouse fill out and sign the Acceptance of Service/Joinder.

3.   File the Petition with county clerk.

4.   Wait 90 days.

5.   Fill out the Decree of Dissolution (divorce), Findings of Fact and Conclusions of Law, and Declaration of Non-Military Service.

6.   Go to court for the hearing and have the Decree of Dissolution (divorce) signed by the judge or court commissioner.

7.   You are then divorced.

b.   IF YOUR SPOUSE IS NOT COOPERATING, OR OBJECTS TO YOUR TERMS

1.   Fill out the Petition and Summons.

2.   File the Petition and Summons with the county clerk.

3.   Have a copy of the Petition and Summons served on your spouse.

4.   After your spouse is served, file the Declaration of Service with the county clerk, or have your spouse sign the Acceptance of Service.

5.   Wait 90 days after the date your spouse is served.

6.   If your spouse has objected and an attorney has filed such objection with the county clerk, find an attorney to represent you.

7.   If no objection has been filed within 90 days, file the default papers and fill out the Findings of Fact, the Declaration of Non-Military Service, and the Decree of Dissolution (divorce).

8.   Go to court for the hearing and have the Decree of Dissolution (divorce) signed by the judge or court commissioner.

9.   You are then divorced.

c.   IF YOUR SPOUSE IS MISSING

1.   Fill out the Petition, the Summons, and the Declaration of Service of Summons by Publication.

2.   File the Petition, the Summons, and the Declaration of Service of Summons by Publication with county clerk.

3.   Fill out the Summons by Publication.

4. Take the Summons to a newspaper for publication once a week for six consecutive weeks.

5. File the Declaration of Publication with the county clerk.

6. Wait 90 days after the date of the first publication of the Summons.

7. If your spouse has objected and an attorney has filed such objection with the county clerk, find an attorney to represent you.

8. If no objection has been filed within 90 days, fill out the Findings of Fact, the Declaration of Non-Military Service, and the Decree of Dissolution (divorce).

9. Go to court for the hearing and have the Decree of Dissolution (divorce) signed by the judge or court commissioner.

10. You are then divorced.

WASHINGTON DIVORCE FORMS

There are two blank tear-out copies of each of the forms necessary for a simple, uncontested divorce where there are no children. One copy of each of the other commonly used forms is provided. Where two copies have been provided (*), please use one as your rough working copy and one for your good copy, which you can then photocopy as necessary for filing. Please see the instructions at the end of chapter 3 if you are typing your own forms. (Note: it may be necessary to make as many as four copies of the Parenting Plan, Form DR 01.0400.) The forms included are:

Petition for Dissolution of Marriage (DR 01.0100)*

Acceptance of Service (DR 01.0310)*

Washington State Child Support Schedule Worksheets

Parenting Plan (DR 01.0400)

Summons (DR 01.0200)

Motion for Default (DR 03.0100)

Order of Default (DR 03.0200)

Declaration in Support of Proposed Parenting Plan (DR 04.0120)

Findings of Fact and Conclusions of Law (DR 04.0300)*

Decree of Dissolution (DR 04.0400)*

Order of Child Support (DR 01.0500)

Declaration of Non-Military Service*

Waiver of Rights under Soldiers and Sailors' Civil Relief Act and Admission of Service

Note (Snohomish County)

Motion and Declaration for Order to Commence and Prosecute Proceeding In Forma Pauperis

Order Authorizing Proceeding In Forma Pauperis

Note: The blank forms included in this half of the book are the most commonly used ones. Blank copies of some other, more specialized forms for unusual situations may be obtained by contacting the clerk of the court or the Office of the Administrator for the Courts at:

Office of the Administrator for the Courts
Temple of Justice, AV-01
Olympia, Washington
98504
(206) 357-2129

WPF DR 01.0100 (8/91)

SUPERIOR COURT OF WASHINGTON
COUNTY OF

In re the Marriage of: ~~Scott McLaughlin~~

Scott McLaughlin   Petitioner
and   Scott M.
Cherie McLaughlin   Respondent.

NO.

PETITION FOR DISSOLUTION
OF MARRIAGE
(PTDSS)

I. BASIS

1.1   This is a petition for dissolution of a marriage which is irretrievably broken.

1.2   The name and last known residence of the wife is:

(first, middle, and last name;   Cherie, Su Fay, McLaughlin
street; city, state, zip)   2723 Linden Lane
                                 Puyallup, WA, 98372

1.3   The name and last known residence of the husband is:

(first, middle, and last name;
street; city, state, zip)

1.4   We were married on 4/15/88 at Puyallup Wash .
                        (Date)   (Place)

1.5   [ ]   Husband and wife are not separated.
      [X]   Husband and wife separated on 11-26-92 .
                                            (Date)

1.6   This court has jurisdiction over my spouse for the reasons which follow.

      [X]   My spouse is presently residing in Washington.
      [ ]   My spouse and I lived in Washington during our marriage and I
            continue to reside in this state.
      [ ]   My spouse and I lived in Washington during our marriage and I
            continue to be a member of the armed forces stationed in this state.
      [ ]   My spouse and I may have conceived a child while within Washington.
      [ ]   My spouse will be personally served in the State of Washington.
      [ ]   My spouse will consent to the jurisdiction of this court.
      [ ]   Other:

PETITION FOR DISSOLUTION OF MARRIAGE
RCW 26.09.020
Page 1

SUPERIOR COURT OF WASHINGTON
COUNTY OF

In re the Marriage of:

Scott McLaughlin   Petitioner

and

Cherie McLaughlin   Respondent.

NO.

PETITION FOR DISSOLUTION
OF MARRIAGE
(PTDSS)

I. BASIS

1.1   This is a petition for dissolution of a marriage which is irretrievably broken.

1.2   The name and last known residence of the wife is:

(first, middle, and last name;
street; city, state, zip)

Cherie, Sufay, McLaughlin
2723 Linden Lane
Puyallup, WA 98372

1.3   The name and last known residence of the husband is:

(first, middle, and last name;
street; city, state, zip)

1.4   We were married on ___4/15/88___ at ___Puyallup Wash___ .
                            (Date)   (Place)

1.5   [ ]   Husband and wife are not separated.
       [X]   Husband and wife separated on ___11/26/92___ .
                                              (Date)

1.6   This court has jurisdiction over my spouse for the reasons which follow.

       [X]   My spouse is presently residing in Washington.
       [ ]   My spouse and I lived in Washington during our marriage and I continue to reside in this state.
       [ ]   My spouse and I lived in Washington during our marriage and I continue to be a member of the armed forces stationed in this state.
       [ ]   My spouse and I may have conceived a child while within Washington.
       [ ]   My spouse will be personally served in the State of Washington.
       [ ]   My spouse will consent to the jurisdiction of this court.
       [ ]   Other:

SELF-COUNSEL PRESS
1704 N. State Street
Bellingham, Washington 98225
FORM USA-D-WASH (1-1)92

1.7 There is community or separate property owned by the parties. The court should make an equitable division of all the property.

[ ] My recommendation for the division of the property will be filed and served at a later date.

[ ] My recommendation for the division of the property is attached.

[X] The property should be divided as described below.

    [X] The wife should be awarded the parties' interest in the following property:

        1974 Jeep wagoneer

        Her Bank account

        1976 Tent Trailer

    [X] The husband should be awarded the parties' interest in the following property:

        1977 Pontiac Fire Bird

        His Bank account

        The Furniture of the home

PETITION FOR DISSOLUTION OF MARRIAGE
RCW 26.09.020
Page 2

SELF-COUNSEL PRESS
1704 N. State Street
Bellingham, Washington 98225
FORM USA-D-WASH (1-2)92

1.7   There is community or separate property owned by the parties. The court should make an equitable division of all the property.

[ ]   My recommendation for the division of the property will be filed and served at a later date.

[ ]   My recommendation for the division of the property is attached.

[X]   The property should be divided as described below.

     [X]   The wife should be awarded the parties' interest in the following property:

1974 Jeep Wagoner
Her bank account
1976 tent trailer

     [X]   The husband should be awarded the parties' interest in the following property:

1977 Poniac Fire Bird
His bank account
The funiture and all household goods
his pension plan

PETITION FOR DISSOLUTION OF MARRIAGE
RCW 26.09.020
Page 2

SELF-COUNSEL PRESS
1704 N. State Street
Bellingham, Washington 98225
FORM USA-D-WASH (1-2)92

2   1.8   DEBTS AND LIABILITIES.

4   [X]   The parties have no debts and liabilities.

       [ ]   The parties have debts and liabilities. The court should make an

6   equitable division of all debts and liabilities.

8   [ ]   My recommendation for the division of the debts and liabilities will be filed and served at a later date.

10   [ ]   My recommendation for the division of the debts and liabilities is attached.

12   [ ]   The debts and liabilities should be divided as described below.

14   [ ]   The wife should be ordered to pay the following debts and liabilities to the following creditors:

16

18

20

22

24

26

28

30   [ ]   The husband should be ordered to pay the following debts and liabilities to the following creditors:

32

34

36

38

40

42

PETITION FOR DISSOLUTION OF MARRIAGE
RCW 26.09.020
Page 3

SELF-COUNSEL PRESS
1704 N. State Street
Bellingham, Washington 98225
FORM USA-D-WASH (1-3)92

1.8   DEBTS AND LIABILITIES.

[X]   The parties have no debts and liabilities.
[ ]   The parties have debts and liabilities. The court should make an equitable division of all debts and liabilities.

[ ]   My recommendation for the division of the debts and liabilities will be filed and served at a later date.
[ ]   My recommendation for the division of the debts and liabilities is attached.
[ ]   The debts and liabilities should be divided as described below.

[ ]   The wife should be ordered to pay the following debts and liabilities to the following creditors:

[ ]   The husband should be ordered to pay the following debts and liabilities to the following creditors:

PETITION FOR DISSOLUTION OF MARRIAGE
RCW 26.09.020
Page 3

SELF-COUNSEL PRESS
1704 N. State Street
Bellingham, Washington 98225
FORM USA-D-WASH (1-3)92

1.9   SPOUSAL MAINTENANCE.

[X]   Spousal maintenance should not be ordered.
[ ]   There is a need for spousal maintenance.

[ ]   The following arrangements for spousal maintenance have been made and [ ] are [ ] are not part of a written separation agreement:

1.10   RESTRAINING ORDER.

[X]   A restraining order should not be ordered.
[ ]   An order should be entered restraining [ ] the husband [ ] the wife [ ] both parties from molesting or disturbing the peace of the other party or of any child because:

1.11   PREGNANCY.

[X]   The wife is not pregnant.
[ ]   The wife is pregnant. The father of the unborn child is [ ] the husband   [ ] not the husband   [ ] unknown.

1.12   DEPENDENT CHILDREN.

[ ]   The parties have no dependent children.
[X]   There are children who are dependent upon either or both spouses. Support for the dependent children should be set pursuant to the Washington State Child Support Schedule. My Parenting Plan for these children:

[X]   is attached and is incorporated by reference as part of this Petition.
[ ]   will be filed and served at a later date pursuant to RCW 26.09.181.

1.9 SPOUSAL MAINTENANCE.

[X] Spousal maintenance should not be ordered.
[ ] There is a need for spousal maintenance.

[ ] The following arrangements for spousal maintenance have been made and [ ] are [ ] are not part of a written separation agreement:

1.10 RESTRAINING ORDER.

[X] A restraining order should not be ordered.
[ ] An order should be entered restraining [ ] the husband [ ] the wife [ ] both parties from molesting or disturbing the peace of the other party or of any child because:

1.11 PREGNANCY.

[X] The wife is not pregnant.
[ ] The wife is pregnant. The father of the unborn child is [ ] the husband [ ] not the husband [ ] unknown.

1.12 DEPENDENT CHILDREN.

[ ] The parties have no dependent children.
[X] There are children who are dependent upon either or both spouses. Support for the dependent children should be set pursuant to the Washington State Child Support Schedule. My Parenting Plan for these children:

[X] is attached and is incorporated by reference as part of this Petition.
[ ] will be filed and served at a later date pursuant to RCW 26.09.181.

PETITION FOR DISSOLUTION OF MARRIAGE
RCW 26.09.020
Page 4

SELF-COUNSEL PRESS
1704 N. State Street
Bellingham, Washington 98225
FORM USA-D-WASH (1-4)92

2 Paragraph 1.12 (continued)

4   Specific Uniform Child Custody Jurisdiction Act information for each
           child is set forth below.   (This information must be provided

6   separately for each child. If there is more than one dependent child,
           you may attach additional copies of this page to this Petition.)

8

           Name of child: Mitchell Mac McLaughlin

10   Date of birth: 9-11-88
           Mother's name: Cherie McLaughlin

12   Father's name: Scott McLaughlin

14   Present address of child: 1030 9th st sw
                                      Puyallup wash

16   98371
           (street,city, state, zip)

18   I [ ] do [X] do not   know of any person other than my spouse who
           has physical custody of this child or claims to have custody or

20   visitation rights with respect to this child.

22   The child has lived in the following places within the last five years
           (list each place, and the names and present addresses of the persons

24   with whom the child lived during that period):
           13202 98 Ave ct E Puyallup wash 98373 Apt(D)

26   Living with Scott McLaughlin and cherie mclaughn
           1030 9th st sw Puyallup wash 98371

28   Living with scott mclaughlin/Julie mclaughlin/william mclaughlin
           Other Legal Proceedings Regarding this Child (RCW 26.27.090):

30

           I [ ] have [X] have not   participated as a party, witness or in any

32   capacity, in any other litigation concerning the custody of this child
           in this state or in any other state.

34

           I [ ] do have   [X] do not have   information of any paternity,

36   dependency, or custody proceeding concerning this child in a court of
           this state or of any other state.

38

           List the county, state and case number of any other legal proceedings:

40

42

PETITION FOR DISSOLUTION OF MARRIAGE
RCW 26.09.020
Page 5

2   Paragraph 1.12 (continued)

4   Specific Uniform Child Custody Jurisdiction Act information for each
           child is set forth below.   (This information must be provided
6   separately for each child. If there is more than one dependent child,
           you may attach additional copies of this page to this Petition.)

8
           Name of child: Heather nikkole mcLaughlin
10   Date of birth: 12/21/89
           Mother's name: Cherie mcLaughlin
12   Father's name: Scott mcLaughlin

14   Present address of child: 1030 9th st sw Payallup wash 98371

16   (street, city, state, zip)

18   I [ ] do [X] do not   know of any person other than my spouse who
           has physical custody of this child or claims to have custody or
20   visitation rights with respect to this child.

22   The child has lived in the following places within the last five years
           (list each place, and the names and present addresses of the persons
24   with whom the child lived during that period):
           13202 96 Ave ct E Puyallup Wash 98373 (Apt D)
26   Lived with Scott mcLaughlin / and Cherie mcLaughlin
           1030 9th st sw Puyallup wash
28   Lived with Scott mcLaughlin / Julie mcLaughlin / William mcLaughlin

           Other Legal Proceedings Regarding this Child (RCW 26.27.090):
30
           I [ ] have [X] have not   participated as a party, witness or in any
32   capacity, in any other litigation concerning the custody of this child
           in this state or in any other state.

34
           I [ ] do have   [X] do not have   information of any paternity,
36   dependency, or custody proceeding concerning this child in a court of
           this state or of any other state.

38
           List the county, state and case number of any other legal proceedings:
40

42

PETITION FOR DISSOLUTION OF MARRIAGE
RCW 26.09.020
Page 5

2   1.13   Other:

4   II.   RELIEF REQUESTED

6   I REQUEST the Court to enter a decree of dissolution.   I also REQUEST the Court to grant the relief described below.

8

      [ ]   Provide reasonable maintenance for the [ ] husband [ ] wife.

10   [X]   Approve my parenting plan for the dependent children.

      [ ]   Determine support for the dependent children pursuant to the Washington

12   State Support Schedule.

      [ ]   Approve the separation agreement.

14   [ ]   Dispose of property and liabilities.

      [X]   Change name of wife to: _*Cherie Dossier*_ .

16   [ ]   Change name of husband to: _____ .

      [ ]   Enter a permanent restraining order.

18   [ ]   Order payment of day care expenses for the children.

      [X]   Award the tax exemptions for the dependent children as follows:

20   *to petitioner*

22

24   [ ]   Order payment of attorney's fees, other professional fees and costs.

      [ ]   Other:

26

      Dated:_____

28   _____

                                  Signature of Lawyer or Petitioner (if petitioner has no lawyer)

30   _____

                                  Print or Type Name (include Washington

32   State Bar Number, if applicable)

34   I declare under penalty of perjury under the laws of the State of Washington that the foregoing is true and correct.

36

      Signed at _____, on _____ .

38   (City and State)   (Date)

40   _____

                                  Signature

42   _____

                                  Print or Type Name

2 | 1.13   Other:

4 | ## II.   RELIEF REQUESTED

6 | I REQUEST the Court to enter a decree of dissolution. I also REQUEST the Court to grant the relief described below.

8 |

[ ]   Provide reasonable maintenance for the [ ] husband [ ] wife.

10 | [X]   Approve my parenting plan for the dependent children.
[ ]   Determine support for the dependent children pursuant to the Washington

12 | State Support Schedule.

[ ]   Approve the separation agreement.

14 | [ ]   Dispose of property and liabilities.

[ ]   Change name of wife to: _____.

16 | [ ]   Change name of husband to: _____.

[ ]   Enter a permanent restraining order.

18 | [ ]   Order payment of day care expenses for the children.

[X]   Award the tax exemptions for the dependent children as follows:

20 |

22 |

24 | [ ]   Order payment of attorney's fees, other professional fees and costs.

[ ]   Other:

26 |

Dated:_____

28 | _____
Signature of Lawyer or Petitioner (if petitioner has no lawyer)

30 |

_____
Print or Type Name (include Washington

32 | State Bar Number, if applicable)

34 | I declare under penalty of perjury under the laws of the State of Washington that the foregoing is true and correct.

36 |

Signed at _____, on _____.

38 | (City and State)   (Date)

40 | _____
Signature

42 | _____
Print or Type Name

PETITION FOR DISSOLUTION OF MARRIAGE
RCW 26.09.020
Page 6

SELF-COUNSEL PRESS
1704 N. State Street
Bellingham, Washington 98225
FORM USA-D-WASH (1-6)92

SUPERIOR COURT OF WASHINGTON
COUNTY OF

In re the Marriage of:

and

                Petitioner

                Respondent.

NO.

[ ] ACCEPTANCE OF SERVICE
    (ACSR)
[ ] NOTICE OF APPEARANCE
    (NTAPR)
[ ] JOINDER
    (JN)

I STATE that:

1.   I am the respondent.

2.   ACCEPTANCE OF SERVICE.

    [ ]   Does not apply.
    [X]   I accept service of:

        [X]   the summons and petition in this action.
        [X]   a parenting plan.
        [ ]   other:

3.   NOTICE OF APPEARANCE.

    [ ]   Does not apply.
    [X]   I enter my appearance, and demand notice of all further proceedings.
        I will inform the clerk of the court of any change in my address. Any
        notices may be sent to me at:

    (street;   2723 Linden Lane
    city, state, zip)   Puyallup, WA 98372

ACCEPTANCE/APPEARANCE/JOINDER
RCW 26.09.030(1)
Page 1

SUPERIOR COURT OF WASHINGTON
COUNTY OF

In re the Marriage of:

Petitioner

and

Respondent.

NO.

[ ] ACCEPTANCE OF SERVICE
   (ACSR)
[ ] NOTICE OF APPEARANCE
   (NTAPR)
[ ] JOINDER
   (JN)

I STATE that:

1.   I am the respondent.

2.   ACCEPTANCE OF SERVICE.

   [ ]   Does not apply.
   [ ]   I accept service of:

      [ ]   the summons and petition in this action.
      [ ]   a parenting plan.
      [ ]   other:

3.   NOTICE OF APPEARANCE.

   [ ]   Does not apply.
   [ ]   I enter my appearance, and demand notice of all further proceedings.
         I will inform the clerk of the court of any change in my address. Any
         notices may be sent to me at:

         (street;
         city, state, zip)

ACCEPTANCE/APPEARANCE/JOINDER
RCW 26.09.030(1)
Page 1

1704 N. State Street
Bellingham, Washington 98225
FORM USA-D-WASH (15-2)92

4. JOINDER.

[ ] Does not apply.
[ ] I join in the petition. I understand that by joining in the petition, I agree with the relief requested in the petition and waive any objections I might have to the allegations of the petition.

I declare under penalty of perjury under the laws of the State of Washington that the foregoing is true and correct.

Signed at _____, on _____.
　　　　　　　　　　(City and State)　　　　　　　　　　　(Date)

　　　　　　　　　　　　　　　　　　_____
　　　　　　　　　　　　　　　　　　　　　　　　Signature

　　　　　　　　　　　　　　　　　　_____
　　　　　　　　　　　　　　　　　　　　Print or Type Name

ACCEPTANCE/APPEARANCE/JOINDER
RCW 26.09.030(1)
Page 2

SELF-COUNSEL PRESS
1704 N. State Street
Bellingham, Washington 98225
FORM USA-D-WASH (15-2)92

2   4.   JOINDER.

4   [ ]   Does not apply.
        [ ]   I join in the petition. I understand that by joining in the petition, I
6   agree with the relief requested in the petition and waive any
               objections I might have to the allegations of the petition.
8

I declare under penalty of perjury under the laws of the State of Washington that
10 the foregoing is true and correct.

12 Signed at _____, on _____.
                       (City and State)   (Date)
14   _____
                                                                  Signature
16   _____
                                                              Print or Type Name
18

ACCEPTANCE/APPEARANCE/JOINDER
RCW 26.09.030(1)
Page 2

SELF-COUNSEL PRESS
1704 N. State Street
Bellingham, Washington 98225
FORM USA-D-WASH (15-2)92

Washington State Child Support Schedule
Worksheets

Mother _____   Father _____

County _____   Superior Court Case Number _____

Children and Ages:			
Part I: Basic Child Support Obligation (See Instructions, Page 5)			
1. Gross Monthly Income		Father	Mother
a. Wages and Salaries		$	$
b. Interest and Dividend Income		$	$
c. Business Income		$	$
d. Spousal Maintenance Received		$	$
e. Other Income		$	$
f. Total Gross Monthly Income (add lines 1a through 1e)		$	$
2. Monthly Deductions from Gross Income			
a. Income Taxes		$	$
b. FICA/Self-Employment Taxes		$	$
c. State Industrial Insurance Deductions		$	$
d. *Mandatory* Union/Professional Dues		$	$
e. Pension Plan Payments		$	$
f. Spousal Maintenance Paid		$	$
g. Normal Business Expenses		$	$
h. Total Deductions from Gross Income (add lines 2a through 2g)		$	$
3. Monthly Net Income (line 1f minus line 2h)		$	$
4. Combined Monthly Net Income (add father's and mother's monthly net incomes from line 3)		$	
5. Basic Child Support Obligation (enter total amount in box ⟶) Child #1 _____ Child #3 _____ Child #2 _____ Child #4 _____		$	
6. Proportional Share of Income (each parent's net income from line 3 divided by line 4)		.	.
7. Each Parent's Basic Child Support Obligation (multiply each number on line 6 by line 5)		$	$
Part II: Health Care, Day Care, and Special Child Rearing Expenses (See Instructions, Page 7)			
8. Health Care Expenses			
a. Monthly Health Insurance Premiums Paid for Child(ren)		$	$
b. Uninsured Monthly Health Care Expenses Paid for Child(ren)		$	$
c. Total Monthly Health Care Expenses (line 8a plus line 8b)		$	$
d. Combined Monthly Health Care Expenses (add father's and mother's totals from line 8c)		$	
e. Maximum Ordinary Monthly Health Care (multiply line 5 times .05)		$	
f. Extraordinary Monthly Health Care Expenses (line 8d minus line 8e, if "0" or negative, enter "0")		$	

Continue to Next Page

Part II: Health Care, Day Care, and Special Child Rearing Expenses (cont.)

9. Day Care and Special Child Rearing Expenses	Father	Mother
a. Day Care Expenses	$	$
b. Education Expenses	$	$
c. Long Distance Transportation Expenses	$	$
d. Other Special Expenses (describe)	$	$
	$	$
	$	$
e. Total Day Care and Special Expenses (add lines 9a through 9d)	$	$
10. Combined Monthly Total of Day Care and Special Expenses (add father's and mother's total day care and special expenses from line 9e)	$	
11. Total Extraordinary Health Care, Day Care, and Special Expenses (line 8f plus line 10)	$	
12. Each Parent's Obligation for Extraordinary Health Care, Day Care, and Special Expenses (multiply each number on line 6 by line 11)	$	$

Part III: Standard Calculation Child Support Obligation

13. Standard Calculation Support Obligation (line 7 plus line 12)	$	$

Part IV: Child Support Credits (See Instructions, Page 8)

14. Child Support Credits		
a. Monthly Health Care Expenses Credit	$	$
b. Day Care and Special Expenses Credit	$	$
c. Other Ordinary Expense Credit (describe)		
	$	$
d. Total Support Credits (add lines 14a through 14c)	$	$

Part V: Net Support Obligation/Presumptive Transfer Payment (See Instructions, Page 8)

15. Net Support Obligation (line 13 minus line 14d)	$	$

Part VI: Additional Factors for Consideration (See Instructions, Page 8)

16. Household Assets (List the estimated present value of all major household assets.)	Father's Household	Mother's Household
a. Real Estate	$	$
b. Stocks and Bonds	$	$
c. Vehicles	$	$
d. Boats	$	$
e. Pensions/IRAs/Bank Accounts	$	$
f. Cash	$	$
g. Insurance Plans	$	$
h. Other (describe)	$	$
	$	$
	$	$
	$	$

Continue to Next Page

17. Household Debt (List liens against household assets, extraordinary debt.)	Father's Household	Mother's Household
	$	$
	$	$
	$	$
	$	$
	$	$
	$	$

18. Other Household Income		
a. Income Of Current Spouse (if not the other parent of this action) Name_____	$	$
Name_____	$	$
b. Income Of Other Adults In Household Name_____	$	$
Name_____	$	$
c. Income Of Children (if considered extraordinary) Name_____	$	$
Name_____	$	$
d. Income From Child Support Name_____	$	$
Name_____	$	$
e. Income From Assistance Programs Program_____	$	$
Program_____	$	$
f. Other Income (describe) _____	$	$
_____	$	$

19. Non-Recurring Income (describe)		
_____	$	$
_____	$	$

20. Child Support Paid For Other Children		
Name/age:_____	$	$
Name/age:_____	$	$

21. Other Children Living In Each Household (First names and ages)		

Continue to Next Page

22. Other Factors For Consideration

Signature and Dates

I declare, under penalty of perjury under the laws of the State of Washington, the information contained in these Worksheets is complete, true, and correct.

_____
Mother's Signature

_____
Father's Signature

_____ _____
Date   City

_____ _____
Date   City

_____
Judge/Reviewing Officer

_____
Date

This worksheet has been certified by the State of Washington Office of the Administrator for the Courts.

Photocopying of the worksheet is permitted.

CHILD SUPPORT ORDER SUMMARY REPORT

Father's Name _____   Mother's Name _____

Cause Number _____   County _____

Date of Order _____   Summary Report Filed By: Father (　)　Mother (　)

1. Type of Order (check one):　　　　　　___ Superior Court　　　　　　___ Administrative Law Judge

2. Was the order for child support (check one):　___ original order for support　　___ order modifying support

3. Number of children of the parties: _____

4. List each child's age below:

　　　Child 1 _____　　　　Child 2 _____　　　　Child 3 _____　　　　Child 4 _____

Complete lines 5-13 using the amounts entered on the child support worksheets signed by the judge/reviewing officer.

5. Father's monthly net income (Support Worksheet page 1, Line 3)　　　　　　　$_____

6. Mother's monthly net income (Support Worksheet page 1, Line 3)　　　　　　　$_____

7. List the basic child support obligation for each child (from Worksheet page 1, Line 5, individual amounts)

　　　Child 1 _____　Child 2 _____　Child 3 _____　Child 4 _____

8. Health Care Expenses (Support Worksheet page 1, Line 8f)　　　　　　　　　　$_____

9. Day Care and Special Expenses (Support Worksheet page 2, Line 9)

　　a. Day Care Expenses　　　　　　　　　　　　　　　　　　　　　　　　　$_____

　　b. Education Expenses　　　　　　　　　　　　　　　　　　　　　　　　　$_____

　　c. Long Distance Transportation Expenses　　　　　　　　　　　　　　　　$_____

　　d. Other_____　　　　　　　　　$_____

　　e. Other_____　　　　　　　　　$_____

10. a. Father's standard calculation support obligation (Support Worksheet page 2, Line 13)　$_____

　　b. Mother's standard calculation support obligation (Support Worksheet page 2, Line 13)　$_____

Actual Transfer Payment Ordered and Deviation (If any)

11. Which Parent is Payor?　　　　Father (　)　　Mother (　)

12. Transfer Payment Amount Ordered By Court　　　　　　　　　　　　　　　$_____

13. a. If the Court deviated (amount from Line 12 differs from amount on Line 10 for the payor), was the
　　　deviation due to: Child Needs (　) Parental Factors (　)

　　b. If the Court deviated, what were the reasons stated by the Court for the deviation?

_____

_____

14. a. Was post-secondary education provided for?　　　　Yes (　)　　　No (　)

　　b. If provided for, was a dollar amount ordered?　　　　Yes (　)　　　No (　)

　　c. If a dollar amount was ordered, enter Payor's amount　　　　　　　　　$_____

Answer remaining questions only if this was an order modifying support.

15. Total amount of the support transfer payment on the previous order?　　　　$_____

16. Which parent paid the transfer payment in the previous order?　　Father (　)　　Mother (　)

17. Was the change in the support transfer payment, if any, phased in? Yes (　)　　　No (　)

18. The change in the support order was due to: (check all applicable categories) Change in residential schedules (　)

　　Change in parent income (　)　　Age of children (　)　　Change in support schedule (　)　　Other (　)

SUPERIOR COURT OF WASHINGTON
COUNTY OF

In re the Marriage of:

Scott McLaughlin   Petitioner
and
Cherie McLaughlin   Respondent.

NO.

PARENTING PLAN
[ ] PROPOSED (PP)
[ ] TEMPORARY (PPT)
[X] FINAL ORDER (PP)

I. GENERAL INFORMATION

1.1   This parenting plan is:

[ ]   the final parenting plan ordered by the court.
[ ]   a temporary parenting plan.
[X]   proposed by _Scott McLaughlin and_____
                          (Name)

1.2   This parenting plan applies to the following children:

Name	Birthdate
Mitchell Mac McLaughlin	9 / 11 / 88
Heather Nikkole McLaughlin	12 / 21 / 89
	/ /
	/ /
	/ /

II. BASIS FOR RESTRICTIONS

2.1   PARENTAL CONDUCT (RCW 26.09.191(1), (2)).

[X]   Does not apply.
[ ]   The [ ] father [ ] mother has engaged in the conduct which follows.

[ ]   Willful abandonment that continues for an extended period of time or substantial refusal to perform parenting functions.
[ ]   Physical, sexual or a pattern of emotional abuse of a child.
[ ]   A history of acts of domestic violence as defined in RCW 26.50.010(1) or an assault or sexual assault which causes grievous bodily harm or the fear of such harm.

PARENTING PLAN
RCW 26.09.181; 187; 194
Page 1

2 2.2   OTHER FACTORS (RCW 26.09.191(3)).

4   ☒   Does not apply.
       [ ]   The [ ] mother's [ ] father's involvement or conduct may have an
6   adverse effect on the child's best interests because of the existence of
             the factors which follow.

8
             [ ]   Neglect or substantial nonperformance of parenting functions.
10   [ ]   A long-term emotional or physical impairment which interferes
                   with the performance of parenting functions as defined in RCW
12   26.09.004.
             [ ]   A long-term impairment resulting from drug, alcohol, or other
14   substance abuse that interferes with the performance of
                   parenting functions.
16   [ ]   The absence or substantial impairment of emotional ties
                   between the parent and child.
18   [ ]   The abusive use of conflict by the parent which creates the
                   danger of serious damage to the child's psychological
20   development.
             [ ]   A parent has withheld from the other parent access to the
22   child for a protracted period without good cause.
             [ ]   Other:
24

26

28

30   These factors [ ] serve ☒ do not serve as a current basis for
             restrictions.
32
                        III. RESIDENTIAL SCHEDULE
34

These provisions set forth where the child(ren) shall reside each day of the year
36 and what contact the child(ren) shall have with each parent.

38 3.1   SCHEDULE FOR HOLIDAYS.

40 The residential schedule for the child(ren) for the holidays listed below is as
    follows:
42

PARENTING PLAN
RCW 26.09.181; 187; 194
Page 2

Paragraph 3.1 (continued)

	With Mother (Specify Whether Odd/Even/Every)	With Father (Specify Whether Odd/Even/Every)
New Year's Day	every	
Martin Luther King Day	—	every
Presidents Day		every
Memorial Day	every	
July 4th	odd	even
Labor Day		every
Veterans Day	—	every
Thanksgiving Day		every
Christmas Eve		every
Christmas Day	odd	even
Easter day		every

[X] For purposes of this parenting plan, a holiday shall begin and end as follows (set forth times):

8:00 am to 4:00 pm

[X] Holidays which fall on a Friday or a Monday shall include Saturday and Sunday. memorial + Labor day only

3.2 PRE-SCHOOL SCHEDULE.

[ ] There are no children of preschool age.

[X] Prior to enrollment in school, the child(ren) shall reside with the [ ] mother [X] father, except for the following days and times when the child(ren) will reside with or be with the other parent:

From _____ to _____
   (Day and Time)   (Day and Time)

From _____ to _____
   (Day and Time)   (Day and Time)

From _____ to _____
   (Day and Time)   (Day and Time)

[X] Detailed description of the pre-school schedule:
2:30 pm - 5:00 pm day care
wednesday

PARENTING PLAN
RCW 26.09.181; 187; 194
Page 3

3.3   SCHOOL SCHEDULE.

Upon enrollment in school, the child(ren) shall reside with the [ ] mother [X] father, except for the following days and times when the child(ren) will reside with or be with the other parent:

From _____ to _____
　　　　　(Day and Time)　　　　　　　　　(Day and Time)

From _____ to _____
　　　　　(Day and Time)　　　　　　　　　(Day and Time)

From _____ to _____
　　　　　(Day and Time)　　　　　　　　　(Day and Time)

[ ]   Detailed description of the school schedule:

[ ]   For purposes of this parenting plan, the school year shall begin and end as follows (set forth times):

3.4   SCHEDULE FOR WINTER VACATION.

The child(ren) shall reside with the [ ] mother [X] father during winter vacation, except for the following days and times when the child(ren) will reside with or be with the other parent:

From _____ to _____
　　　　　(Day and Time)　　　　　　　　　(Day and Time)

From _____ to _____
　　　　　(Day and Time)　　　　　　　　　(Day and Time)

[ ]   Detailed description of the schedule for winter vacation:

PARENTING PLAN
RCW 26.09.181; 187; 194
Page 4

SELF-COUNSEL PRESS
1704 N. State Street
Bellingham, Washington 98225
FORM USA-D-WASH (2-4)92

SELF-COUNSEL PRESS
1704 N. State Street
Bellingham, Washington 98225
FORM USA-D-WASH (2-5)92

3.5   SCHEDULE FOR SPRING VACATION.

The child(ren) shall reside with the [ ] mother [X] father during spring vacation, except for the following days and times when the child(ren) will reside with or be with the other parent:

From _____ to _____
              (Day and Time)   (Day and Time)
From _____ to _____
              (Day and Time)   (Day and Time)

[ ]   Detailed description of the schedule for spring vacation:

3.6   SUMMER SCHEDULE.

Upon completion of the school year, the child(ren) shall reside with the [ ] mother [X] father, except for the following days and times when the child(ren) will reside with or be with the other parent:

From _____ to _____
              (Day and Time)   (Day and Time)
From _____ to _____
              (Day and Time)   (Day and Time)
From _____ to _____
              (Day and Time)   (Day and Time)

[ ]   Detailed description of the schedule for the summer:

PARENTING PLAN
RCW 26.09.181; 187; 194
Page 5

2 3.7 VACATION WITH PARENTS.

4   [ ]   Does not apply.
       [X]   The schedule for vacation with parents is as follows:

6   one week per year with a
                    30 day notice. Up to three
8   weeks with a 60 day notice.

10 3.8 SCHEDULE FOR SPECIAL OCCASIONS.

12   The residential schedule for the child(ren) for the following special occasions
       (i.e., birthdays) is as follows :

	With Mother (Specify Whether Odd/Even/Every)	With Father (Specify Whether Odd/Even/Every)
Mother's Day	every	
Father's Day		every
Mother's Birthday	every	
Father's Birthday		every
Chinese New Year	every	
daughters birthday		every
sons birthday		every

30 3.9 PRIORITIES UNDER THE RESIDENTIAL SCHEDULE.

32   [ ]   Does not apply.
       [X]   For purposes of this parenting plan the following days shall have
34   priority:

36   [ ]   Parent's vacation over holidays, other special occasions and
                  the residential schedule for school vacations. Holidays over
38   other special occasions and the residential schedule for school
                  vacations. Special occasions over the residential schedule for
40   school vacations.
           [X]   Other: X Parent's vacation over
42   holidays.

PARENTING PLAN
RCW 26.09.181; 187; 194
Page 6

SELF-COUNSEL PRESS
1704 N. State Street
Bellingham, Washington 98225
FORM USA-D-WASH (2-6)92

2 3.10 RESTRICTIONS.

4 [ ] Does not apply.
   [X] The following restrictions shall apply when the child(ren) spend(s)
6 time with the [X] mother [X] father (see paragraph 2.1):

8 Can not take Childern out of
   State without written permission.

10

12

3.11 TRANSPORTATION ARRANGEMENTS.
14
Transportation arrangements for the child(ren), other than costs, between
16 parents shall be as follows:

18

20

22

24 3.12 DESIGNATION OF CUSTODIAN.

26 The children named in this parenting plan are scheduled to reside the
   majority of the time with the [ ] mother [X] father. This parent is
28 designated the custodian of the child(ren) solely for purposes of all other
   state and federal statutes which require a designation or determination of
30 custody. This designation shall not affect either parent's rights and
   responsibilities under this parenting plan.

32
3.13 OTHER:
34

36

38

40

42

PARENTING PLAN
RCW 26.09.181; 187; 194
Page 7

SELF-COUNSEL PRESS
1704 N. State Street
Bellingham, Washington 98225
FORM USA-D-WASH (2-7)92

IV. DECISION MAKING

4.1 Each parent shall make decisions regarding the day-to-day care and control of each child while the child is residing with that parent, except as provided below.

4.2 Decisions regarding each child shall be made as follows:

Education decisions   [ ] mother [X] father [ ] joint
Non-emergency health care [ ] mother [X] father [ ] joint
Religious upbringing   [ ] mother [ ] father [X] joint
_____ [ ] mother [ ] father [ ] joint
_____ [ ] mother [ ] father [ ] joint
_____ [ ] mother [ ] father [ ] joint
_____ [ ] mother [ ] father [ ] joint

4.3 RESTRICTIONS.

[X]   Does not apply.
[ ]   Sole decision making shall be ordered to the [ ] mother [ ] father for the following reasons:

    [ ]   A limitation on the other parent's decision-making authority is mandated by RCW 26.09.191.
    [ ]   Both parents are opposed to mutual decision making.
    [ ]   One parent is opposed to mutual decision making, and such opposition is reasonably based on the following criteria:

        (a)   The existence of a limitation under RCW 26.09.191;
        (b)   The history of participation of each parent in decision making in each of the areas in RCW 26.09.184(4)(a);
        (c)   Whether the parents have demonstrated ability and desire to cooperate with one another in decision making in each of the areas in RCW 26.09.184(4)(a); and
        (d)   The parents' geographic proximity to one another, to the extent that it effects their ability to make timely mutual decisions.

V. DISPUTE RESOLUTION

[ ]   No dispute resolution process, except court action, shall be ordered, because [ ] a limiting factor under RCW 26.09.191 applies or [ ] one parent is unable to afford the cost of the proposed dispute resolution process.

[ ]   Disputes between the parties shall be submitted to (list person or agency):

    [ ]   counseling by _____, or
    [ ]   mediation by _____, or
    [ ]   arbitration by _____.

The cost of this process shall be allocated between the parties as follows:

    [ ]   _____% mother _____% father.
    [ ]   based on each party's proportional share of income from line 6 of the child support worksheets.
    [ ]   as determined in the dispute resolution process.

The counseling, mediation or arbitration process shall be commenced by notifying the other party by [ ] written request [ ] certified mail [ ] other:

In the dispute resolution process:

(a)   Preference shall be given to carrying out this Parenting Plan.
(b)   Unless an emergency exists, the parents shall use the designated process to resolve disputes relating to implementation of the plan, except those related to financial support.
(c)   A written record shall be prepared of any agreement reached in counseling or mediation and of each arbitration award and shall be provided to each party.
(d)   If the court finds that a parent has used or frustrated the dispute resolution process without good reason, the court shall award attorneys' fees and financial sanctions to the other parent.
(e)   The parties have the right of review from the dispute resolution process to the superior court.

PARENTING PLAN
RCW 26.09.181; 187; 194
Page 9

VI. OTHER PROVISIONS

[ ] There are no other provisions.
[ ] There are the following other provisions:

VII. DECLARATION

I declare under penalty of perjury under the laws of the State of Washington that this plan has been proposed in good faith and that the statements in Part II of this Plan are true and correct.

_____   _____
              Mother   Date and Place of Signature

_____   _____
              Father   Date and Place of Signature

SELF-COUNSEL PRESS
1704 N. State Street
Bellingham, Washington 98225
FORM USA-D-WASH (2-10)92

VIII. ORDER BY THE COURT

WARNING: Violation of residential provisions of this order with actual knowledge of its terms is punishable by contempt of court and may be a criminal offense under RCW 9A.40.070(2). Violation of this order may subject a violator to arrest.

When mutual decision making is designated but cannot be achieved, the parties shall make a good faith effort to resolve the issue through the dispute resolution process.

If a parent fails to comply with a provision of this plan, the other parent's obligations under the plan are not affected.

The parenting plan set forth above is adopted and approved as an order of this court.

Dated: _____   _____

                                                    Judge/Commissioner

Presented by: Approved for entry:

_____   _____

Signature and Washington State Bar   Signature and Washington State Bar
Number, if applicable   Number, if applicable

SUPERIOR COURT OF WASHINGTON
COUNTY OF

In re the Marriage of:

                        Petitioner

and

                        Respondent.

NO.

SUMMONS
(SM)

TO THE RESPONDENT:

1.   The petitioner has started an action in the above court requesting:

        [ ]   that your marriage be dissolved.
        [ ]   a legal separation.
        [ ]   that your marriage be declared invalid.

    Additional requests, if any, are stated in the petition, a copy of which is attached to this summons.

2.   You must respond to this summons and petition by serving a copy of your written response on the person signing this summons and by filing the original with the clerk of the court. If you do not serve your written response within 20 days (or 60 days if you are served outside of the State of Washington) after the date this summons was served on you, exclusive of the day of service, the court may enter an order of default against you, and at the end of 90 days after service and filing, the court may, without further notice to you, enter a decree and approve or provide for the relief requested in the petition. If you serve a notice of appearance on the undersigned person, you are entitled to notice before an order of default or a decree may be entered.

3.   Your written response to the summons and petition must be on forms approved by the Office of the Administrator for the Courts. These forms may be obtained by contacting the clerk of the court, or by contacting the Office of the Administrator for the Courts at:

        Office of the Administrator for the Courts
        Temple of Justice, AV-01
        Olympia, Washington 98504
        (206) 357-2129

4. If this action has not been filed with the court, you may demand that the petitioner file this action with the court. If you do so, the demand must be in writing and must be served upon the person signing this summons. Within 14 days after you serve the demand, the petitioner must file this action with the court, or the service on you of this summons and petition will be void.

5. If you wish to seek the advice of an attorney in this matter, you should do so promptly so that your written response, if any, may be served on time.

6. One method of serving a copy of your response on the petitioner is to send it by certified mail with return receipt requested.

This summons is issued pursuant to Superior Court Civil Rule 4.1 of the State of Washington.

Dated:_____

_____
Signature of Lawyer or Petitioner (if petitioner has no lawyer)

_____
Print or Type Name (include Washington State Bar Number, if applicable)

FILE ORIGINAL WITH THE CLERK OF THE COURT AT:

SERVE A COPY OF YOUR RESPONSE ON:

[ ] Petitioner
[ ] Petitioner's Lawyer

_____
(Name of Court)

_____
(Name)

_____
(Address)

_____
(Address)

Phone: _____

SUMMONS
CR 4.1
Page 2

SUPERIOR COURT OF WASHINGTON
COUNTY OF

In re the Marriage of:

Petitioner

and

Respondent.

NO.

MOTION FOR DEFAULT
(MTDFL)

I. MOTION

The petitioner moves the court for an order of default. Venue of this action is proper as set forth in the Declaration below.

Dated:_____

_____
Signature of Lawyer or Moving Party (if party has no lawyer)

_____
Print or Type Name (include Washington State Bar Number, if applicable)

II. DECLARATION

2.1   The court has proper jurisdiction and venue pursuant to the allegations of the petition at the time of filing.

The petitioner resides in _____.
(County and State)

The child(ren) reside(s) in _____.
(County and State)

Respondent resides in _____.
(County and State)

[ ]   Other:

MOTION FOR DEFAULT
CR 55(a); RCW 26.09.030
Page 1

2 2.2 This court has jurisdiction over the respondent for the reasons which
       follow.

4

6   [ ]   The respondent is presently residing in Washington.
       [ ]   The respondent and I lived in Washington during our marriage and
             I continue to reside in this state.

8   [ ]   The respondent and I lived in Washington during our marriage and
             I continue to be a member of the armed forces stationed in this
10   state.
       [ ]   The respondent and I may have conceived a child while within
12   Washington.
       [ ]   The respondent was personally served in the State of Washington.
14   [ ]   The respondent agreed to submit to the jurisdiction of this court.

16 2.3 Respondent was served with petition on _____ in _____.
                                                (Date)   (State)
18

    2.4 More than twenty days have elapsed, if served within the State of
20   Washington, or sixty days have elapsed, if served outside of the State of
         Washington, since the date of service.

22

    2.5 [ ]   Respondent has failed to appear.
24   [ ]   Respondent has appeared, but has failed to respond.

26 2.6 Respondent is not on active duty in the U.S. armed forces.

28 2.7 Other:

30

32 I declare under penalty of perjury under the laws of the State of Washington
    that the foregoing is true and correct.

34

    Signed at _____, on _____.
36   (City and State)   (Date)

38   _____
                                                    Signature

40   _____
                                      Print or Type Name and Washington
42   State Bar Number, if applicable

MOTION FOR DEFAULT
CR 55(a); RCW 26.09.030
Page 2

WPF DR 03.0200 (7/91)

SUPERIOR COURT OF WASHINGTON
COUNTY OF

In re the Marriage of:

Petitioner

and

Respondent.

NO.

ORDER OF DEFAULT
(ORDFL)

I. BASIS

A motion for default against the respondent has been presented.

II. FINDINGS

The Court FINDS that:

2.1   The court has proper jurisdiction and venue.

2.2   The respondent was served with petition, summons, a proposed parenting plan, if any, and _____ on _____.

(Date)

2.3   More than twenty days have elapsed, if served within the State of Washington, or sixty days have elapsed, if served outside the State of Washington, since the date of service.

2.4   [ ]   The respondent has failed to appear.
       [ ]   The respondent has appeared but has failed to respond.

III. ORDER

IT IS ORDERED that the respondent is in default.

Dated: _____   _____

                                          Judge/Commissioner

Presented by:

_____
Signature and Washington State Bar
Number, if applicable

ORDER OF DEFAULT
CR 55(a); RCW 26.09.030
Page 1

SELF-COUNSEL PRESS
1704 N. State Street
Bellingham, Washington 98225
FORM USA-D-WASH (7-1)92

SUPERIOR COURT OF WASHINGTON
COUNTY OF

In re the Marriage of:

                                        Petitioner

and

                                        Respondent.

NO.

DECLARATION IN SUPPORT OF PROPOSED TEMPORARY PARENTING PLAN

(DCLR)

(COMPLETE A SEPARATE FORM FOR EACH CHILD IF NECESSARY)

This declaration is made by the [ ] father [ ] mother.

1. _____ has resided with the
                    (Name of Child)
   following persons during the past twelve months:

Name	Address	Length of Time Child Resided With This Person

2.   (a)   The mother's performance of parenting functions relating to the daily needs of the child during the past twelve months:

     (b)   The mother's work schedule for the past twelve months:

     (c)   The mother's current work schedule:

DECLARATION RE PROPOSED TEMPORARY PLAN
RCW 26.09.194(1)
Page 1

SELF-COUNSEL PRESS
1704 N. State Street
Bellingham, Washington 98225
FORM USA-D-WASH (8-1)92

3.   (a)   The father's performance of parenting functions relating to the daily needs of the child during the past twelve months:

        (b)   The father's work schedule for the past twelve months:

        (c)   The father's current work schedule:

4.   (a)   The child-care schedule for the past twelve months:

        (b)   The current child-care schedule:

5.   Any circumstances under RCW 26.09.191 that are likely to pose a serious risk to the child(ren) and that warrant limitation on the award to a parent of temporary residence or time with the child(ren) pending entry of a permanent parenting plan are set forth in Part II of my proposed temporary parenting plan.

I declare under penalty of perjury under the laws of the State of Washington that the foregoing is true and correct.

Signed at _____, on _____.
                    (City and State)   (Date)

                                    _____
                                        Signature

                                    _____
                                      Print or Type Name

DECLARATION RE PROPOSED TEMPORARY PLAN
RCW 26.09.194(1)
Page 2

SUPERIOR COURT OF WASHINGTON
COUNTY OF

In re the Marriage of:

Petitioner

and

Respondent.

NO.

**FINDINGS OF FACT AND
CONCLUSIONS OF LAW
(FNFCL)**

I. HEARING/TRIAL

1.1   A hearing was held on _____.
            (Date)

1.2   The findings are based on:

        [ ]   trial.
        [ ]   agreement.
        [ ]   an order of default entered on _____.
                                                    (Date)

1.3   The following people attended:

        [ ]   Petitioner:
        [ ]   Petitioner's Lawyer:
        [ ]   Respondent:
        [ ]   Respondent's Lawyer:
        [ ]   Other:

II. FINDINGS OF FACT

Upon the basis of the court record, the court FINDS:

2.1   The petitioner is a resident of the State of Washington or is a member of
        the armed forces and is stationed in this state.

2.2   The court has subject matter jurisdiction over the marriage. The respondent

        [ ]   appeared or responded.
        [ ]   was served in the following manner:

FINDINGS OF FACT AND CONCLUSIONS OF LAW
CR 52; RCW 26.09.030; .070(3)
Page 1

SUPERIOR COURT OF WASHINGTON
COUNTY OF

In re the Marriage of:

	NO.
Petitioner	**FINDINGS OF FACT AND CONCLUSIONS OF LAW**
and	**(FNFCL)**
Respondent.	

I. HEARING/TRIAL

1.1   A hearing was held on _____.
(Date)

1.2   The findings are based on:

[ ]   trial.
[ ]   agreement.
[ ]   an order of default entered on _____.
(Date)

1.3   The following people attended:

[ ]   Petitioner:
[ ]   Petitioner's Lawyer:
[ ]   Respondent:
[ ]   Respondent's Lawyer:
[ ]   Other:

II. FINDINGS OF FACT

Upon the basis of the court record, the court FINDS:

2.1   The petitioner is a resident of the State of Washington or is a member of the armed forces and is stationed in this state.

2.2   The court has subject matter jurisdiction over the marriage. The respondent

[ ]   appeared or responded.
[ ]   was served in the following manner:

FINDINGS OF FACT AND CONCLUSIONS OF LAW
CR 52; RCW 26.09.030; .070(3)
Page 1

2.3   BASIS OF JURISDICTION OVER THE RESPONDENT.

[ ]   There are no facts to establish personal jurisdiction over the respondent.

[ ]   The facts below establish personal jurisdiction over the respondent.

    [ ]   The respondent is presently residing in Washington.

    [ ]   The parties lived in Washington during their marriage and the petitioner continues to reside in this state.

    [ ]   The parties lived in Washington during their marriage and the petitioner continues to be a member of the armed forces stationed in this state.

    [ ]   The parties may have conceived a child while within Washington.

    [ ]   The respondent was served within the State of Washington.

    [ ]   The petitioner resides in Washington and the respondent consents to jurisdiction.

    [ ]   Other:

2.4   The parties were married on _____ at _____.
                                   (Date)   (Place)

2.5   STATUS OF THE PARTIES.

[ ]   Husband and wife are not separated.

[ ]   Husband and wife separated on _____.
                                             (Date)

2.6   STATUS OF THE MARRIAGE.

[ ]   The marriage is irretrievably broken and at least 90 days have elapsed since the date the petition was filed and since the date the summons was served or the respondent joined.

[ ]   The petitioner wishes to be legally separated.

[ ]   The petitioner is petitioning for a declaration concerning the invalidity of the marriage. The court FINDS the following facts concerning the validity of the marriage:

FINDINGS OF FACT AND CONCLUSIONS OF LAW
CR 52; RCW 26.09.030; .070(3)
Page 2

2 2.3 BASIS OF JURISDICTION OVER THE RESPONDENT.

4 [ ] There are no facts to establish personal jurisdiction over the respondent.

6 [ ] The facts below establish personal jurisdiction over the respondent.

8 [ ] The respondent is presently residing in Washington.
   [ ] The parties lived in Washington during their marriage and the petitioner continues to reside in this state.
10
   [ ] The parties lived in Washington during their marriage and the petitioner continues to be a member of the armed forces stationed in this state.
12

14 [ ] The parties may have conceived a child while within Washington.

16 [ ] The respondent was served within the State of Washington.
   [ ] The petitioner resides in Washington and the respondent consents to jurisdiction.
18
   [ ] Other:

20

22 2.4 The parties were married on _____ at _____.
                                      (Date)   (Place)

24 2.5 STATUS OF THE PARTIES.

26 [ ] Husband and wife are not separated.
   [ ] Husband and wife separated on _____.
28   (Date)

30 2.6 STATUS OF THE MARRIAGE.

32 [ ] The marriage is irretrievably broken and at least 90 days have elapsed since the date the petition was filed and since the date the summons was served or the respondent joined.
34
   [ ] The petitioner wishes to be legally separated.
36 [ ] The petitioner is petitioning for a declaration concerning the invalidity of the marriage. The court FINDS the following facts concerning the
38 validity of the marriage:

40

42

FINDINGS OF FACT AND CONCLUSIONS OF LAW
CR 52; RCW 26.09.030; .070(3)
Page 2

SELF-COUNSEL PRESS
1704 N. State Street
Bellingham, Washington 98225
FORM USA-D-WASH (9-2)92

2   2.7   SEPARATION CONTRACT.

4   [ ]   There is no written separation contract or prenuptial agreement.
    [ ]   A written separation contract or prenuptial agreement was executed
6   on _____ and is filed herein.
                (Date)

8
          [ ]   The separation contract [ ] was [ ] was not fair when executed.
10   [ ]   The separation contract [ ] should [ ] should not be approved.

12 2.8   COMMUNITY PROPERTY.

14 [ ]   The parties do not have community property.
    [ ]   The parties have community property as set forth in Exhibit ____.
16   This exhibit is attached or filed and incorporated by reference as part
          of these findings.
18 [ ]   The parties have the following community property:

20

22

24

26

28

30

32

34

36

38

40

42

FINDINGS OF FACT AND CONCLUSIONS OF LAW
CR 52; RCW 26.09.030; .070(3)
Page 3

2   2.7   SEPARATION CONTRACT.

4   [ ]   There is no written separation contract or prenuptial agreement.
    [ ]   A written separation contract or prenuptial agreement was executed
6   on _____ and is filed herein.
                    (Date)

8
    [ ]   The separation contract [ ] was [ ] was not fair when executed.
10 [ ]   The separation contract [ ] should [ ] should not be approved.

12 2.8   COMMUNITY PROPERTY.

14 [ ]   The parties do not have community property.
    [ ]   The parties have community property as set forth in Exhibit ____.
16   This exhibit is attached or filed and incorporated by reference as part
          of these findings.
18 [ ]   The parties have the following community property:

20

22

24

26

28

30

32

34

36

38

40

42

FINDINGS OF FACT AND CONCLUSIONS OF LAW
CR 52; RCW 26.09.030; .070(3)
Page 3

SELF-COUNSEL PRESS
1704 N. State Street
Bellingham, Washington 98225
FORM USA-D-WASH (9-3)92

2

2.9   HUSBAND'S SEPARATE PROPERTY.

4   [ ]   The husband has no separate property.
       [ ]   The husband has separate property as set forth in Exhibit ___. This
6   exhibit is attached or filed and incorporated by reference as part of
               these findings.
8   [ ]   The husband has the following separate property:

10

12

14

16

18

20

22

24   2.10   WIFE'S SEPARATE PROPERTY.

26   [ ]   The wife has no separate property.
       [ ]   The wife has separate property as set forth in Exhibit ___. This
28   exhibit is attached or filed and incorporated by reference as part of
               these findings.
30   [ ]   The wife has the following separate property:

32

34

36

38

40

42

FINDINGS OF FACT AND CONCLUSIONS OF LAW
CR 52; RCW 26.09.030; .070(3)
Page 4

2.9   HUSBAND'S SEPARATE PROPERTY.

[ ]   The husband has no separate property.

[ ]   The husband has separate property as set forth in Exhibit ___. This exhibit is attached or filed and incorporated by reference as part of these findings.

[ ]   The husband has the following separate property:

2.10   WIFE'S SEPARATE PROPERTY.

[ ]   The wife has no separate property.

[ ]   The wife has separate property as set forth in Exhibit ____. This exhibit is attached or filed and incorporated by reference as part of these findings.

[ ]   The wife has the following separate property:

FINDINGS OF FACT AND CONCLUSIONS OF LAW
CR 52; RCW 26.09.030; .070(3)
Page 4

SELF-COUNSEL PRESS
1704 N. State Street
Bellingham, Washington 98225
FORM USA-D-WASH (9-4)92

2.11 COMMUNITY DEBTS AND OTHER LIABILITIES.

[ ]   There are no known community obligations.

[ ]   The parties have incurred community debts and liabilities as set forth in Exhibit ___. This exhibit is attached or filed and incorporated by reference as part of these findings.

[ ]   The parties have incurred the following community debts and liabilities:

<u>Creditor</u>   <u>Amount</u>

2.12 HUSBAND'S SEPARATE DEBTS AND OTHER LIABILITIES.

[ ]   The husband has no known separate obligations.

[ ]   The husband has incurred separate debts and liabilities as set forth in Exhibit ___. This exhibit is attached or filed and incorporated by reference as part of these findings.

[ ]   The husband has incurred the following separate debts and liabilities:

<u>Creditor</u>   <u>Amount</u>

FINDINGS OF FACT AND CONCLUSIONS OF LAW
CR 52; RCW 26.09.030; .070(3)
Page 5

2.11   COMMUNITY DEBTS AND OTHER LIABILITIES.

[ ]   There are no known community obligations.
[ ]   The parties have incurred community debts and liabilities as set forth in Exhibit ___. This exhibit is attached or filed and incorporated by reference as part of these findings.
[ ]   The parties have incurred the following community debts and liabilities:

<u>Creditor</u>   <u>Amount</u>

2.12   HUSBAND'S SEPARATE DEBTS AND OTHER LIABILITIES.

[ ]   The husband has no known separate obligations.
[ ]   The husband has incurred separate debts and liabilities as set forth in Exhibit ___. This exhibit is attached or filed and incorporated by reference as part of these findings.
[ ]   The husband has incurred the following separate debts and liabilities:

<u>Creditor</u>   <u>Amount</u>

2.13   WIFE'S SEPARATE DEBTS AND OTHER LIABILITIES.

[ ]   The wife has no known separate obligations.

[ ]   The wife has incurred separate debts and liabilities as set forth in Exhibit ___. This exhibit is attached or filed and incorporated by reference as part of these findings.

[ ]   The wife has incurred the following separate debts and liabilities:

<u>Creditor</u>   <u>Amount</u>

2.14   NEED FOR MAINTENANCE.

[ ]   Neither party is in need of maintenance.

[ ]   The [ ] husband [ ] wife is in need of spousal maintenance. This finding is based upon the following factors:

[ ]   The party seeking maintenance is unable to meet his or her needs independently.

[ ]   The time necessary to acquire sufficient education or training to enable the party seeking maintenance to find employment appropriate to his or her skill, interests, style of life and other attendant circumstances.

[ ]   The standard of living established during the marriage.

[ ]   The duration of the marriage.

[ ]   The age, physical and emotional condition, and financial obligations of the party seeking maintenance.

SELF-COUNSEL PRESS
1704 N. State Street
Bellingham, Washington 98225
FORM USA-D-WASH (9-6)92

2 2.13 WIFE'S SEPARATE DEBTS AND OTHER LIABILITIES.

4   [ ]   The wife has no known separate obligations.
       [ ]   The wife has incurred separate debts and liabilities as set forth
6   in Exhibit ___. This exhibit is attached or filed and incorporated by
              reference as part of these findings.
8   [ ]   The wife has incurred the following separate debts and liabilities:

10   Creditor   Amount

12

14

16

18

20

22

24

26

28 2.14 NEED FOR MAINTENANCE.

       [ ]   Neither party is in need of maintenance.
30   [ ]   The [ ] husband [ ] wife is in need of spousal maintenance. This
              finding is based upon the following factors:
32

              [ ]   The party seeking maintenance is unable to meet his or her
34   needs independently.
              [ ]   The time necessary to acquire sufficient education or training
36   to enable the party seeking maintenance to find employment
                     appropriate to his or her skill, interests, style of life and other
38   attendant circumstances.
              [ ]   The standard of living established during the marriage.
40   [ ]   The duration of the marriage.
              [ ]   The age, physical and emotional condition, and financial
42   obligations of the party seeking maintenance.

FINDINGS OF FACT AND CONCLUSIONS OF LAW
CR 52; RCW 26.09.030; .070(3)
Page 6

SELF-COUNSEL PRESS
1704 N. State Street
Bellingham, Washington 98225
FORM USA-D-WASH (9-6)92

2 | Paragraph 2.14 (continued)

4 | [ ] The past, present and future earning or economic capacity of each spouse, including the earning or economic capacity of
6 | each spouse that was enhanced, diminished or foregone during the marriage.
8 | [ ] The standard of living each spouse will experience after dissolution of the marriage.
10 | [ ] The ability of the spouse from whom maintenance is sought to meet his or her needs and financial obligations while meeting
12 | those of the spouse seeking maintenance.
 | [ ] A lack of work history, education or training.
14 | [ ] Other:

16 |

 | 2.15 ABILITY TO PAY MAINTENANCE.
18 |

 | [ ] Does not apply.
20 | [ ] The [ ] husband [ ] wife has the ability to pay maintenance as follows:

22 |

24 |

26 |

28 |

30 | 2.16 RESTRAINING ORDER.

32 | [ ] Does not apply.
 | [ ] A continuing restraining order against the [ ] husband [ ] wife
34 | [ ] both parties is necessary because:

36 |

38 |

40 |

42 |

FINDINGS OF FACT AND CONCLUSIONS OF LAW
CR 52; RCW 26.09.030; .070(3)
Page 7

2 | Paragraph 2.14 (continued)

4   [ ]   The past, present and future earning or economic capacity of each spouse, including the earning or economic capacity of
6   each spouse that was enhanced, diminished or foregone during the marriage.

8   [ ]   The standard of living each spouse will experience after dissolution of the marriage.

10   [ ]   The ability of the spouse from whom maintenance is sought to meet his or her needs and financial obligations while meeting
12   those of the spouse seeking maintenance.

         [ ]   A lack of work history, education or training.

14   [ ]   Other:

16

2.15 ABILITY TO PAY MAINTENANCE.

18

         [ ]   Does not apply.
20   [ ]   The [ ] husband   [ ] wife has the ability to pay maintenance as follows:

22

24

26

28

2.16 RESTRAINING ORDER.

30

32   [ ]   Does not apply.
         [ ]   A continuing restraining order against the [ ] husband [ ] wife
34   [ ] both parties is necessary because:

36

38

40

42

FINDINGS OF FACT AND CONCLUSIONS OF LAW
CR 52; RCW 26.09.030; .070(3)
Page 7

SELF-COUNSEL PRESS
1704 N. State Street
Bellingham, Washington 98225
FORM USA-D-WASH (9-7)92

2 | 2.17 COURT COSTS AND FEES.

4 | [ ] Does not apply.
[ ] The following court costs and fees have been incurred in this action:

6

8

10

12

14

2.18 ATTORNEY'S FEES AND COSTS.

16

[ ] Does not apply.
18 | [ ] Each of the parties has sufficient property, income or resources available to pay his or her own respective attorney fees and costs.
20 | [ ] The [ ] husband [ ] wife has incurred reasonable attorney fees and costs in the amount of $ _____. The other spouse has the ability
22 | to pay these fees and the [ ] husband [ ] wife has the need for the payment of these fees as follows:

24

26

28

30

32 | 2.19 PREGNANCY.

34 | [ ] The wife is not pregnant.
[ ] The wife is pregnant. The father of the unborn child is [ ] the
36 | husband [ ] not the husband [ ] unknown.

38 | 2.20 DEPENDENT CHILDREN.

40 | [ ] The parties have no dependent children.
[ ] The parties have children who are dependent or partially dependent
42 | upon either or both spouses.

FINDINGS OF FACT AND CONCLUSIONS OF LAW
CR 52; RCW 26.09.030; .070(3)
Page 8

2

2.17 COURT COSTS AND FEES.

4
[ ]   Does not apply.
[ ]   The following court costs and fees have been incurred in this action:

6

8

10

12

14

2.18 ATTORNEY'S FEES AND COSTS.

16
[ ]   Does not apply.

18
[ ]   Each of the parties has sufficient property, income or resources available to pay his or her own respective attorney fees and costs.

20
[ ]   The [ ] husband [ ] wife has incurred reasonable attorney fees and costs in the amount of $ _____. The other spouse has the ability

22
to pay these fees and the [ ] husband [ ] wife has the need for the payment of these fees as follows:

24

26

28

30

32

2.19 PREGNANCY.

34
[ ]   The wife is not pregnant.

36
[ ]   The wife is pregnant. The father of the unborn child is [ ] the husband [ ] not the husband [ ] unknown.

38

2.20 DEPENDENT CHILDREN.

40
[ ]   The parties have no dependent children.

42
[ ]   The parties have children who are dependent or partially dependent upon either or both spouses.

SELF-COUNSEL PRESS
1704 N. State Street
Bellingham, Washington 98225
FORM USA-D-WASH (9-8)92

2.21 JURISDICTION OVER THE CHILDREN.

[ ] Does not apply.
[ ] This court does not have jurisdiction over the children.
[ ] This court has jurisdiction over the children for the reasons set forth below.

[ ] This state is the home state of the child because

[ ] the child lived in Washington with a parent or a person acting as a parent for at least six consecutive months immediately preceding the commencement of this proceeding.
[ ] the child is less than six months old and has lived in Washington with a parent or a person acting as parent since birth.
[ ] any absences from Washington have been only temporary.
[ ] Washington was the home state of the child within six months before the commencement of this proceeding and the child's absence from the state is because of removal or retention by a person claiming custody or for other reasons.

[ ] It is in the best interest of the child that this court assume jurisdiction because the child and the parents or the child and at least one contestant have significant connection with the state; there is substantial evidence concerning the child's present or future care, protection, training and personal relationships in the state; and

[ ] the child has no home state elsewhere.
[ ] the child's home state has declined to exercise jurisdiction.

[ ] The child is physically present in this state and has been abandoned or it is necessary in an emergency to protect the child because he or she has been subjected to or threatened with mistreatment or abuse.

FINDINGS OF FACT AND CONCLUSIONS OF LAW
CR 52; RCW 26.09.030; .070(3)
Page 9

SELF-COUNSEL PRESS
1704 N. State Street
Bellingham, Washington 98225
FORM USA-D-WASH (9-9)92

2.21 JURISDICTION OVER THE CHILDREN.

[ ] Does not apply.
[ ] This court does not have jurisdiction over the children.
[ ] This court has jurisdiction over the children for the reasons set forth below.

    [ ] This state is the home state of the child because

        [ ] the child lived in Washington with a parent or a person acting as a parent for at least six consecutive months immediately preceding the commencement of this proceeding.

        [ ] the child is less than six months old and has lived in Washington with a parent or a person acting as parent since birth.

        [ ] any absences from Washington have been only temporary.

        [ ] Washington was the home state of the child within six months before the commencement of this proceeding and the child's absence from the state is because of removal or retention by a person claiming custody or for other reasons.

    [ ] It is in the best interest of the child that this court assume jurisdiction because the child and the parents or the child and at least one contestant have significant connection with the state; there is substantial evidence concerning the child's present or future care, protection, training and personal relationships in the state; and

        [ ] the child has no home state elsewhere.
        [ ] the child's home state has declined to exercise jurisdiction.

    [ ] The child is physically present in this state and has been abandoned or it is necessary in an emergency to protect the child because he or she has been subjected to or threatened with mistreatment or abuse.

FINDINGS OF FACT AND CONCLUSIONS OF LAW
CR 52; RCW 26.09.030; .070(3)
Page 9

SELF-COUNSEL PRESS
1704 N. State Street
Bellingham, Washington 98225
FORM USA-D-WASH (9-9)92

2 | Paragraph 2.21 (continued)

4   [ ]   No other state has jurisdiction or a state with jurisdiction has declined to exercise jurisdiction on the ground that this state

6   is the more appropriate forum and it is in the best interest of the child for this court to assume jurisdiction.

8   [ ]   This court has continuing jurisdiction because the court has previously made a child custody or parenting plan

10   determination in this matter and Washington remains the residence of the children or any contestant.

12   [ ]   Other:

14

16

2.24 PARENTING PLAN.

18

     [ ]   Does not apply.

20   [ ]   The attached or filed Parenting Plan signed by the court is approved and incorporated as part of these findings.

22

2.25 CHILD SUPPORT.

24

     [ ]   Does not apply.

26   [ ]   There are children in need of support and child support should be set pursuant to the Washington State Child Support Schedule.

28

2.26 OTHER:

30

32

34

36

38

40

42

FINDINGS OF FACT AND CONCLUSIONS OF LAW
CR 52; RCW 26.09.030; .070(3)
Page 10

2 | Paragraph 2.21 (continued)

4   [ ]   No other state has jurisdiction or a state with jurisdiction has declined to exercise jurisdiction on the ground that this state

6   is the more appropriate forum and it is in the best interest of the child for this court to assume jurisdiction.

8   [ ]   This court has continuing jurisdiction because the court has previously made a child custody or parenting plan

10   determination. in this matter and Washington remains the residence of the children or any contestant.

12   [ ]   Other:

14

16

18   **2.24   PARENTING PLAN.**

         [ ]   Does not apply.

20   [ ]   The attached or filed Parenting Plan signed by the court is approved and incorporated as part of these findings.

22

   2.25   CHILD SUPPORT.

24

         [ ]   Does not apply.

26   [ ]   There are children in need of support and child support should be set pursuant to the Washington State Child Support Schedule.

28

   2.26   OTHER:

30

32

34

36

38

40

42

FINDINGS OF FACT AND CONCLUSIONS OF LAW
CR 52; RCW 26.09.030; .070(3)
Page 10

SELF-COUNSEL PRESS
1704 N. State Street
Bellingham, Washington 98225
FORM USA-D-WASH (9-10)92

III. CONCLUSIONS OF LAW

The court makes the following conclusions of law from the foregoing findings of fact:

3.1   The court has jurisdiction over the:

[ ]   parties
[ ]   subject matter
[ ]   property and obligations

3.2   The parties should be granted a decree:

[ ]   of dissolution.
[ ]   of legal separation.
[ ]   declaring the marriage invalid.
[ ]   declaring the marriage valid.

3.3   The court has disposed of the property, liabilities, fees, costs, made a parenting plan and provision for support of the child(ren), if any, and maintenance, if any, all in an equitable manner.

3.4   PROPERTY TO BE AWARDED THE HUSBAND.

[ ]   Does not apply.
[ ]   The husband should be awarded as his separate property the property set forth in Exhibit _____. This exhibit is attached or filed and incorporated by reference as part of these findings.
[ ]   The husband should be awarded as his separate property the following property (list real estate, furniture, vehicles, pensions, insurance, bank accounts, etc.):

FINDINGS OF FACT AND CONCLUSIONS OF LAW
CR 52; RCW 26.09.030; .070(3)
Page 11

SELF-COUNSEL PRESS
1704 N. State Street
Bellingham, Washington 98225
FORM USA-D-WASH (9-11)92

III. CONCLUSIONS OF LAW

The court makes the following conclusions of law from the foregoing findings of fact:

3.1   The court has jurisdiction over the:

    [ ]   parties
    [ ]   subject matter
    [ ]   property and obligations

3.2   The parties should be granted a decree:

    [ ]   of dissolution.
    [ ]   of legal separation.
    [ ]   declaring the marriage invalid.
    [ ]   declaring the marriage valid.

3.3   The court has disposed of the property, liabilities, fees, costs, made a parenting plan and provision for support of the child(ren), if any, and maintenance, if any, all in an equitable manner.

3.4   PROPERTY TO BE AWARDED THE HUSBAND.

    [ ]   Does not apply.
    [ ]   The husband should be awarded as his separate property the property set forth in Exhibit _____. This exhibit is attached or filed and incorporated by reference as part of these findings.
    [ ]   The husband should be awarded as his separate property the following property (list real estate, furniture, vehicles, pensions, insurance, bank accounts, etc.):

FINDINGS OF FACT AND CONCLUSIONS OF LAW
CR 52; RCW 26.09.030; .070(3)
Page 11

3.5   PROPERTY TO BE AWARDED TO THE WIFE.

[ ]   Does not apply.

[ ]   The wife should be awarded as her separate property the property set forth in Exhibit _____. This exhibit is attached or filed and incorporated by reference as part of these findings.

[ ]   The wife should be awarded as her separate property the following property (list real estate, furniture, vehicles, pensions, insurance, bank accounts, etc.):

3.6   OBLIGATIONS TO BE PAID BY THE HUSBAND.

[ ]   Does not apply.

[ ]   The husband should pay the community or separate obligations as set forth in Exhibit _____. This exhibit is attached or filed and incorporated by reference as part of these findings.

[ ]   The husband should pay the following community or separate obligations:

Creditor   Amount

FINDINGS OF FACT AND CONCLUSIONS OF LAW
CR 52; RCW 26.09.030; .070(3)
Page 12

SELF-COUNSEL PRESS
1704 N. State Street
Bellingham, Washington 98225
FORM USA-D-WASH (9-12)92

3.5   PROPERTY TO BE AWARDED TO THE WIFE.

[ ]   Does not apply.

[ ]   The wife should be awarded as her separate property the property set forth in Exhibit _____. This exhibit is attached or filed and incorporated by reference as part of these findings.

[ ]   The wife should be awarded as her separate property the following property (list real estate, furniture, vehicles, pensions, insurance, bank accounts, etc.):

3.6   OBLIGATIONS TO BE PAID BY THE HUSBAND.

[ ]   Does not apply.

[ ]   The husband should pay the community or separate obligations as set forth in Exhibit _____. This exhibit is attached or filed and incorporated by reference as part of these findings.

[ ]   The husband should pay the following community or separate obligations:

Creditor   Amount

3.7   OBLIGATIONS TO BE PAID BY THE WIFE.

[ ]   Does not apply.

[ ]   The wife should pay the community or separate obligations as set forth in Exhibit _____.   This exhibit is attached or filed and incorporated by reference as part of these findings.

[ ]   The wife should pay the following community or separate obligations:

Creditor   Amount

3.8   NAME CHANGES.

[ ]   Does not apply.

[ ]   The wife's name should be changed to _____.
                                                              (Name)

[ ]   The husband's name should be changed to _____.
                                                              (Name)

3.9   RESTRAINING ORDER.

[ ]   Does not apply.

[ ]   A continuing restraining order should be entered as follows:

FINDINGS OF FACT AND CONCLUSIONS OF LAW
CR 52; RCW 26.09.030; .070(3)
Page 13

2 3.7 OBLIGATIONS TO BE PAID BY THE WIFE.

4 [ ] Does not apply.
   [ ] The wife should pay the community or separate obligations as set
6   forth in Exhibit _____. This exhibit is attached or filed and
        incorporated by reference as part of these findings.
8 [ ] The wife should pay the following community or separate obligations:

10   Creditor   Amount

12

14

16

18

20

22

   3.8 NAME CHANGES.
24
   [ ] Does not apply.
26 [ ] The wife's name should be changed to _____.
                                              (Name)
28 [ ] The husband's name should be changed to _____.
                                                 (Name)
30 3.9 RESTRAINING ORDER.

32 [ ] Does not apply.
   [ ] A continuing restraining order should be entered as follows:
34

36

38

40

42

FINDINGS OF FACT AND CONCLUSIONS OF LAW
CR 52; RCW 26.09.030; .070(3)
Page 13

SELF-COUNSEL PRESS
1704 N. State Street
Bellingham, Washington 98225
FORM USA-D-WASH (9-13)92

3.10   ATTORNEY'S FEES AND COSTS.

[ ]   Does not apply.
[ ]   Attorney's fees, other professional fees and costs should be paid as
         follows:

3.11   OTHER:

Dated: _____

_____
Judge/Commissioner

Presented by:

Approved for entry:
Notice of presentation waived:

_____
Signature and Washington State Bar
Number, if applicable

_____
Signature and Washington State Bar
Number, if applicable

FINDINGS OF FACT AND CONCLUSIONS OF LAW
CR 52; RCW 26.09.030; .070(3)
Page 14

2 | 3.10   ATTORNEY'S FEES AND COSTS.

4 | [ ]   Does not apply.
    | [ ]   Attorney's fees, other professional fees and costs should be paid as
6 | follows:

8 |

10 |

12 | 3.11   OTHER:

14 |

16 |

18 |

20 |

22 |

24 |

26 |

28 |

30 |

32 |

    | Dated: _____   _____
34 | Judge/Commissioner

36 | Presented by: Approved for entry:
    | Notice of presentation waived:
38 |

40 | _____   _____
    | Signature and Washington State Bar   Signature and Washington State Bar
42 | Number, if applicable   Number, if applicable

FINDINGS OF FACT AND CONCLUSIONS OF LAW
CR 52; RCW 26.09.030; .070(3)
Page 14

SUPERIOR COURT OF WASHINGTON
COUNTY OF

In re the Marriage of:

Petitioner

and

Respondent.

NO.

DECREE OF DISSOLUTION/
LEGAL SEPARATION/
CONCERNING VALIDITY
(DCD) or (DCLGSP) or (DCINMG)
[ ] CLERK'S ACTION REQUIRED
(See paragraph 3.11)

I. JUDGMENT SUMMARY

A. Judgment Creditor _____

B. Judgment Debtor _____

C. Principal judgment amount (back support) $ _____
from _____ to _____.
(Date)   (Date)

D. Interest to date of Judgment . . . . $ _____

E. Attorney's fees . . . . $ _____

F. Costs . . . . $ _____

G. Other recovery amount. . . . . $ _____

H. Principal judgment shall bear interest at _____% per annum.

I. Attorney's fees, costs and other recovery
amounts shall bear interest at . . . . . . _____% per annum.

J. Attorney for Judgment Creditor _____

K. Attorney for Judgment Debtor _____

II. BASIS

The findings of fact and conclusions of law have been entered in this case.

III. DECREE

IT IS DECREED that:

3.1 STATUS OF THE MARRIAGE.

[ ] The marriage of the parties is dissolved.
[ ] The husband and wife are legally separated.
[ ] The marriage of the parties is invalid as of _____.
(Date)

[ ] The marriage of the parties is valid.

DECREE
RCW 26.09.030; .040; .070(3)
Page 1

SUPERIOR COURT OF WASHINGTON
COUNTY OF

In re the Marriage of:

Petitioner

and

Respondent.

NO.
DECREE OF DISSOLUTION/
LEGAL SEPARATION/
CONCERNING VALIDITY
(DCD) or (DCLGSP) or (DCINMG)
[ ] CLERK'S ACTION REQUIRED
(See paragraph 3.11)

I. JUDGMENT SUMMARY

A. Judgment Creditor _____

B. Judgment Debtor _____

C. Principal judgment amount (back support) $ _____
   from _____ to _____.
   (Date)   (Date)

D. Interest to date of Judgment . . . . $ _____

E. Attorney's fees . . . . $ _____

F. Costs . . . . $ _____

G. Other recovery amount. . . . . $ _____

H. Principal judgment shall bear interest at _____% per annum.

I. Attorney's fees, costs and other recovery
   amounts shall bear interest at . . . . . . _____% per annum.

J. Attorney for Judgment Creditor _____

K. Attorney for Judgment Debtor _____

II. BASIS

The findings of fact and conclusions of law have been entered in this case.

III. DECREE

IT IS DECREED that:

3.1 STATUS OF THE MARRIAGE.

[ ] The marriage of the parties is dissolved.
[ ] The husband and wife are legally separated.
[ ] The marriage of the parties is invalid as of _____.
   (Date)

[ ] The marriage of the parties is valid.

DECREE
RCW 26.09.030; .040; .070(3)
Page 1

SELF-COUNSEL PRESS
1704 N. State Street
Bellingham, Washington 98225
FORM USA-D-WASH (10-2)92

3.2   PARENTING PLAN.

[ ]   Does not apply.
[ ]   The parties shall comply with the Parenting Plan signed by the court, which is attached or filed. The Parenting Plan signed by the court is approved and incorporated as part of this decree.

3.3   CHILD SUPPORT.

[ ]   Does not apply.
[ ]   Child support shall be paid in accordance with the order of child support signed by the court, which is attached or filed. This order is incorporated as part of this decree.

3.4   PROPERTY TO BE AWARDED THE HUSBAND.

[ ]   Does not apply.
[ ]   The husband is awarded as his separate property the property set forth in Exhibit _____. This exhibit is attached or filed and incorporated by reference as part of this decree.
[ ]   The husband is awarded as his separate property the following property (list real estate, furniture, vehicles, pensions, insurance, bank accounts, etc.):

DECREE
RCW 26.09.030; .040; .070(3)
Page 2

2   3.2   PARENTING PLAN.

4   [ ]   Does not apply.
           [ ]   The parties shall comply with the Parenting Plan signed by the court,
6   which is attached or filed. The Parenting Plan signed by the court is
                 approved and incorporated as part of this decree.

8

     3.3   CHILD SUPPORT.

10
           [ ]   Does not apply.
12   [ ]   Child support shall be paid in accordance with the order of child
                 support signed by the court, which is attached or filed.   This order
14   is incorporated as part of this decree.

16   3.4   PROPERTY TO BE AWARDED THE HUSBAND.

18   [ ]   Does not apply.
           [ ]   The husband is awarded as his separate property the property set
20   forth in Exhibit _____.   This exhibit is attached or filed and
                 incorporated by reference as part of this decree.
22   [ ]   The husband is awarded as his separate property the following
                 property (list real estate, furniture, vehicles, pensions, insurance, bank
24   accounts, etc.):

26

28

30

32

34

36

38

40

42

DECREE
RCW 26.09.030; .040; .070(3)
Page 2

2   3.5   PROPERTY TO BE AWARDED TO THE WIFE.

4   [ ]   Does not apply.

         [ ]   The wife is awarded as her separate property the property set forth

6   in Exhibit ___. This exhibit is attached or filed and incorporated by reference as part of this decree.

8   [ ]   The wife is awarded as her separate property the following property (list real estate, furniture, vehicles, pensions, insurance, bank accounts,

10   etc.):

12

14

16

18

20

22

24

26

28

30

32

34

36

38

40

42

DECREE
RCW 26.09.030; .040; .070(3)
Page 3

2 | 3.5   PROPERTY TO BE AWARDED TO THE WIFE.

4   [ ]   Does not apply.

       [ ]   The wife is awarded as her separate property the property set forth

6   in Exhibit ___. This exhibit is attached or filed and incorporated by reference as part of this decree.

8   [ ]   The wife is awarded as her separate property the following property (list real estate, furniture, vehicles, pensions, insurance, bank accounts,

10   etc.):

12

14

16

18

20

22

24

26

28

30

32

34

36

38

40

42

DECREE
RCW 26.09.030; .040; .070(3)
Page 3

2   3.6   OBLIGATIONS TO BE PAID BY THE HUSBAND.

4   [ ]   Does not apply.
          [ ]   The husband shall pay the community or separate obligations set
6   forth in Exhibit _____.   This exhibit is attached or filed and
                 incorporated by reference as part of this decree.
8   [ ]   The husband shall pay the following community or separate
                 obligations:

10
                          Creditor   Amount
12

14

16

18

20

22

24

26

28

30

32

34

36

38

40

42

DECREE
RCW 26.09.030; .040; .070(3)
Page 4

2   3.6   OBLIGATIONS TO BE PAID BY THE HUSBAND.

4   [ ]   Does not apply.

[ ]   The husband shall pay the community or separate obligations set
6   forth in Exhibit _____.   This exhibit is attached or filed and
incorporated by reference as part of this decree.

8   [ ]   The husband shall pay the following community or separate
obligations:

10

                                     <u>Creditor</u>   <u>Amount</u>

12

14

16

18

20

22

24

26

28

30

32

34

36

38

40

42

DECREE
RCW 26.09.030; .040; .070(3)
Page 4

2 3.7   OBLIGATIONS TO BE PAID BY THE WIFE.

4   [ ]   Does not apply.
         [ ]   The wife shall pay the community or separate obligations set forth
6   in Exhibit ___.   This exhibit is attached or filed and incorporated by
                reference as part of this decree.
8   [ ]   The wife shall pay the following community or separate obligations:

10   <u>Creditor</u>   <u>Amount</u>

12

14

16

18

20

22

24

26

28

30

32

34

       3.8   HOLD HARMLESS PROVISION.
36
         [ ]   Does not apply.
38   [ ]   Each party is required to pay all debt incurred since the date of
                separation and to hold the other party harmless from any collection
40   action relating to separate or community debt, including reasonable
                attorney's fees and costs incurred in defending against any attempts
42   to collect an obligation of the other party.

DECREE
RCW 26.09.030; .040; .070(3)
Page 5

SELF-COUNSEL PRESS
1704 N. State Street
Bellingham, Washington 98225
FORM USA-D-WASH (10-5)92

3.7 OBLIGATIONS TO BE PAID BY THE WIFE.

[ ] Does not apply.

[ ] The wife shall pay the community or separate obligations set forth in Exhibit ___. This exhibit is attached or filed and incorporated by reference as part of this decree.

[ ] The wife shall pay the following community or separate obligations:

<u>Creditor</u>   <u>Amount</u>

3.8 HOLD HARMLESS PROVISION.

[ ] Does not apply.

[ ] Each party is required to pay all debt incurred since the date of separation and to hold the other party harmless from any collection action relating to separate or community debt, including reasonable attorney's fees and costs incurred in defending against any attempts to collect an obligation of the other party.

DECREE
RCW 26.09.030; .040; .070(3)
Page 5

SELF-COUNSEL PRESS
1704 N. State Street
Bellingham, Washington 98225
FORM USA-D-WASH (10-5)92

2   3.9   SPOUSAL MAINTENANCE.

4   [ ]   Does not apply.

        [ ]   The [ ] husband [ ] wife shall pay maintenance as set forth in Exhibit

6   _____. This exhibit is attached or filed and incorporated by reference as part of this decree.

8   [ ]   The [ ] husband [ ] wife shall pay $ _____ maintenance. Maintenance shall be paid [ ] weekly [ ] semi-monthly [ ] monthly.

10   The first maintenance payment shall be due on _____. The

                                               (Date)

12   obligation to pay future maintenance is terminated:

14   [ ]   upon the death of either party or the remarriage of the party receiving maintenenance.

16   [ ]   Other:

18

20

           Payments shall be made:

22

            [ ]   directly to the other spouse.

24   [ ]   to the Washington State Support Registry (only available if child support is ordered).

26   [ ]   to the clerk of this court as trustee for remittance to the other spouse (only available if there are no dependent children).

28

       [ ]   If a spousal maintenance payment is more than fifteen days past due

30   and the total of such past due payments is equal to or greater than one hundred dollars, or if the obligor requests a withdrawal of

32   accumulated contributions from the Department of Retirement Systems, the obligee may seek a mandatory benefits assignment order

34   under Chapter 41.50 RCW without prior notice to the obligor.

        [ ]   The Department of Retirement Systems may make a direct payment

36   of all or part of a withdrawal of accumulated contributions pursuant to RCW 41.50.550(3).

38   [ ]   Other:

40

42

DECREE
RCW 26.09.030; .040; .070(3)
Page 6

3.9   SPOUSAL MAINTENANCE.

[ ]   Does not apply.

[ ]   The [ ] husband [ ] wife shall pay maintenance as set forth in Exhibit
       ____. This exhibit is attached or filed and incorporated by reference
       as part of this decree.

[ ]   The [ ] husband [ ] wife shall pay $ _____ maintenance.
       Maintenance shall be paid [ ] weekly [ ] semi-monthly [ ] monthly.
       The first maintenance payment shall be due on _____. The
                                                         (Date)
       obligation to pay future maintenance is terminated:

       [ ]   upon the death of either party or the remarriage of the party
              receiving maintenenance.
       [ ]   Other:

Payments shall be made:

       [ ]   directly to the other spouse.
       [ ]   to the Washington State Support Registry (only available if
              child support is ordered).
       [ ]   to the clerk of this court as trustee for remittance to the other
              spouse (only available if there are no dependent children).

[ ]   If a spousal maintenance payment is more than fifteen days past due
       and the total of such past due payments is equal to or greater than
       one hundred dollars, or if the obligor requests a withdrawal of
       accumulated contributions from the Department of Retirement
       Systems, the obligee may seek a mandatory benefits assignment order
       under Chapter 41.50 RCW without prior notice to the obligor.
[ ]   The Department of Retirement Systems may make a direct payment
       of all or part of a withdrawal of accumulated contributions pursuant
       to RCW 41.50.550(3).
[ ]   Other:

DECREE
RCW 26.09.030; .040; .070(3)
Page 6

2   3.10   NAME CHANGES.

4   [ ]   Does not apply.

      [ ]   The wife's name shall be changed to _____.

6   (Name)

      [ ]   The husband's name shall be changed to _____.

8   (Name)

10   3.11   CONTINUING RESTRAINING ORDER.

12   [ ]   Does not apply.

      [ ]   A continuing restraining order is entered as follows:

14

16   [ ]   Each party is restrained from assaulting, harassing, molesting or disturbing the peace of the other party.*

          [ ]   Each party is restrained from entering the home of the other

18   party.*

20   ***VIOLATION OF THE ABOVE PROVISIONS OF THIS ORDER WITH ACTUAL NOTICE OF THEIR TERMS IS A**

22   **CRIMINAL OFFENSE UNDER CHAPTER 26.09 RCW, AND WILL SUBJECT THE VIOLATOR TO ARREST. RCW**

24   **26.09.060.**

          [ ]   Other:

26

28

30

32   This order shall be filed forthwith in the clerk's office and entered of record.

34   The clerk of the court shall forward a copy of this order on or before the next judicial day, to _____.

36   (Name of law enforcement agency)

38   _____ shall forthwith enter this order

      (Name of law enforcement agency)

40   into any computer-based criminal intelligence system available in this state used by law enforcement agencies to list outstanding warrants.

42

3.10   NAME CHANGES.

[ ]   Does not apply.
[ ]   The wife's name shall be changed to _____.
　　　　　　　　　　　　　　　　　　　　　　　　　(Name)
[ ]   The husband's name shall be changed to _____.
　　　　　　　　　　　　　　　　　　　　　　　　　(Name)

3.11   CONTINUING RESTRAINING ORDER.

[ ]   Does not apply.
[ ]   A continuing restraining order is entered as follows:

　　　[ ]   Each party is restrained from assaulting, harassing, molesting
　　　　　　 or disturbing the peace of the other party.*
　　　[ ]   Each party is restrained from entering the home of the other
　　　　　　 party.*

　　　***VIOLATION OF THE ABOVE PROVISIONS OF THIS
　　　ORDER WITH ACTUAL NOTICE OF THEIR TERMS IS A
　　　CRIMINAL OFFENSE UNDER CHAPTER 26.09 RCW, AND
　　　WILL SUBJECT THE VIOLATOR TO ARREST.   RCW
　　　26.09.060.**
　　　[ ]   Other:

This order shall be filed forthwith in the clerk's office and entered of record.

The clerk of the court shall forward a copy of this order on or before the next judicial day, to _____.
　　　　　　　　　　　　　　(Name of law enforcement agency)

_____ shall forthwith enter this order
(Name of law enforcement agency)
into any computer-based criminal intelligence system available in this state used by law enforcement agencies to list outstanding warrants.

DECREE
RCW 26.09.030; .040; .070(3)
Page 7

3.12 ATTORNEY'S FEES, OTHER PROFESSIONAL FEES AND COSTS.

[ ] Does not apply.
[ ] Attorney's fees, other professional fees and costs shall be paid as follows:

3.13 OTHER:

Dated: _____   _____
                                            Judge/Commissioner

Presented by: Approved for entry:
                                        Notice of presentation waived:

_____   _____
Signature and Washington State Bar   Signature and Washington State Bar
Number, if applicable   Number, if applicable

DECREE
RCW 26.09.030; .040; .070(3)
Page 8

3.12 ATTORNEY'S FEES, OTHER PROFESSIONAL FEES AND COSTS.

[ ]   Does not apply.
[ ]   Attorney's fees, other professional fees and costs shall be paid as follows:

3.13 OTHER:

Dated: _____   _____
                                                          Judge/Commissioner

Presented by: Approved for entry:
                                            Notice of presentation waived:

_____   _____
Signature and Washington State Bar   Signature and Washington State Bar
Number, if applicable   Number, if applicable

DECREE
RCW 26.09.030; .040; .070(3)
Page 8

SELF-COUNSEL PRESS
1704 N. State Street
Bellingham, Washington 98225
FORM USA-D-WASH (10-8)92

SUPERIOR COURT OF WASHINGTON
COUNTY OF

In re:

                                    Petitioner

and

                                    Respondent.

NO.

ORDER OF CHILD SUPPORT
(ORS)

I. JUDGMENT SUMMARY

A. Judgment Creditor _____

B. Judgment Debtor _____

C. Principal judgment amount (back support) $ _____

from _____ to _____.
         (Date)   (Date)

D. Interest to date of Judgment . . . . $ _____

E. Attorney's fees . . . . $ _____

F. Costs . . . . $ _____

G. Other recovery amount. . . . . $ _____

H. Principal judgment shall bear interest at _____ % per annum.

I. Attorney's fees, costs and other recovery
    amounts shall bear interest at . . . . . _____ % per annum.

J. Attorney for Judgment Creditor _____

K. Attorney for Judgment Debtor _____

II. BASIS

2.1 This order is entered pursuant to a:

[ ] decree of dissolution, legal separation or a declaration of invalidity.
[ ] finding of parentage.
[ ] petition for modification of child support.
[ ] temporary order.
[ ] other:

2.2 The child support worksheet(s) which are initialed by the court are attached
     or filed and are incorporated by reference.

ORDER OF CHILD SUPPORT
RCW 26.09.175; 26.26.132(5)
Page 1

III. ORDER

IT IS ORDERED that:

3.1 CHILDREN FOR WHOM SUPPORT IS REQUIRED.

Name	Date of Birth	Soc. Sec. Number
_____	_____	_____
_____	_____	_____
_____	_____	_____
_____	_____	_____
_____	_____	_____
_____	_____	_____

3.2 PERSON PAYING SUPPORT (OBLIGOR).

Name:
Address:

Soc.Sec.Num:
Employer and Address:

[ ] Monthly Net Income: $ _____
[ ] The income of the obligor is imputed at $ _____
because:

    [ ] the obligor's income is unknown.
    [ ] the obligor is voluntarily unemployed.
    [ ] the obligor is voluntarily underemployed.

ORDER OF CHILD SUPPORT
RCW 26.09.175; 26.26.132(5)
Page 2

SELF-COUNSEL PRESS
1704 N. State Street
Bellingham, Washington 98225
FORM USA-D-WASH (11-2)92

3.3 PERSON RECEIVING SUPPORT (OBLIGEE).

Name:
Address:

Soc.Sec.Num:
Employer:

[ ] Monthly Net Income: $ _____
[ ] The income of the obligee is imputed at $ _____
     because:

     [ ]   the obligee's income is unknown.
     [ ]   the obligee is voluntarily unemployed.
     [ ]   the obligee is voluntarily underemployed.

The parent receiving support may be required to submit an accounting of
how the support is being spent to benefit the child.

3.4 TRANSFER PAYMENT (check one of the boxes below).

[ ] The obligor parent shall pay $ _____ per month.
[ ] The obligor parent shall pay the following amounts per month for the
     following children:

Name	Amount
_____	$ _____
_____	$ _____
_____	$ _____
_____	$ _____
_____	$ _____
_____	$ _____
TOTAL MONTHLY AMOUNT	$ _____

3.5 STANDARD CALCULATION.

$ _____ per month. (See Worksheet A, line 15.)

ORDER OF CHILD SUPPORT
RCW 26.09.175; 26.26.132(5)
Page 3

SELF-COUNSEL PRESS
1704 N. State Street
Bellingham, Washington 98225
FORM USA-D-WASH (11-3)92

2   3.6   REASONS FOR DEVIATION FROM STANDARD CALCULATION.

4   [ ]   The child support amount ordered in paragraph 3.4 does not deviate from the standard calculation.

6   [ ]   The child support amount ordered in paragraph 3.4 deviates from the standard calculation for the following reasons:

8

[ ]   Income of a new spouse;
10   [ ]   Income of other adults in the household;
[ ]   Child support actually received from other relationships;
12   [ ]   Gifts;
[ ]   Prizes;
14   [ ]   Possession of wealth;
[ ]   Extraordinary income of a child;
16   [ ]   Tax planning which results in greater benefit to the children;
[ ]   A nonrecurring source of income;
18   [ ]   Payment would reduce the parent's income level below the DSHS need standard;
20   [ ]   Extraordinary debt not voluntarily incurred;
[ ]   A significant disparity in the living costs of the parents due to
22   conditions beyond their control;
[ ]   Special needs of disabled children;
24   [ ]   Special medical, educational, or psychological needs of the children;
26   [ ]   The child spends a significant amount of time with the parent who is obligated to make a support transfer payment;
28   [ ]   Children from other relationships;
[ ]   Other:

30

The factual basis for these reasons is as follows:

32

34

36

38

40

42

ORDER OF CHILD SUPPORT
RCW 26.09.175; 26.26.132(5)
Page 4

3.7 REASONS WHY REQUEST FOR DEVIATION WAS DENIED.

[ ] Does not apply.
[ ] The deviation sought by the [ ] obligor [ ] obligee was denied because:

    [ ] no good reason exists to justify deviation.
    [ ] other:

3.8 STARTING DATE AND DAY TO BE PAID.

Starting Date:
Day(s) of the month support is due:

[ ] This is a modification of child support pursuant to RCW 26.09.170 (8)(a) and (d) and the child support obligation set forth in Paragraph 3.4 shall be implemented in two equal increments as follows:

ORDER OF CHILD SUPPORT
RCW 26.09.175; 26.26.132(5)
Page 5

3.9   HOW SUPPORT PAYMENTS SHALL BE MADE.

Support payments shall be made:

[ ]   to the Washington State Support Registry
P.O. Box 9009
Olympia, WA 98507
Phone: 1-800-922-4306

[ ]   A notice of payroll deduction may be issued or other income withholding action under Chapter 26.18 RCW or Chapter 74.20A RCW may be taken, without further notice to the obligor parent at any time after entry of an order by the court.

[ ]   Wage withholding, by notice of payroll deduction or other income withholding action under Chapter 26.18 RCW or Chapter 74.20A RCW, without further notice to the obligor, is delayed until a payment is past due, because:

[ ]   there is good cause not to require immediate income withholding.

[ ]   the parties have reached a written agreement which the court approves that provides for an alternative arrangement. (See below).

Each party shall notify the Washington State Support Registry of any change in residence address.

[ ]   pursuant to the following alternative payment plan:

A notice of payroll deduction may issue or other income withholding action may be taken under RCW 26.18 or RCW 74.20A without prior notice to the obligor:

[ ]   if a support payment is past due.
[ ]   at any time.

The order may be submitted to the Washington State Support Registry for enforcement if a support payment is past due.

ORDER OF CHILD SUPPORT
RCW 26.09.175; 26.26.132(5)
Page 6

3.10 TERMINATION OF SUPPORT.

Support shall be paid:

[ ]   until a permanent child support order is entered by this court.

[ ]   until the child(ren) reach(es) the age of 18, except as otherwise provided below in Paragraph 3.10.

[ ]   until the child(ren) reach(es) the age of 18 or completes high school, whichever occurs last, except as otherwise provided below in Paragraph 3.10.

[ ]   after the age of 18 for _____
                                                                (Name)
        who is a dependnent adult child, until the child is capable of self-support and the necessity for support ceases.

[ ]   until the obligation for post secondary support set forth in Paragraph 3.10 begins for the child(ren).

[ ]   other:

3.11 POST SECONDARY EDUCATIONAL SUPPORT.

[ ]   Does not apply.

[ ]   The parents shall pay for the post secondary educational support of the child(ren) as follows:

3.12 DIRECT PAYMENT TO THIRD PARTIES FOR EXPENSES NOT INCLUDED IN THE TRANSFER PAYMENT.

[ ] Does not apply.

[ ] The mother shall pay _____ % and the father _____% of the following expenses incurred on behalf of the children listed in Paragraph 3.1:

    [ ] day care.
    [ ] educational expenses.
    [ ] long distance transportation expenses.
    [ ] other:

[ ] The obligor shall pay the following amounts each month the expense is incurred on behalf of the children listed in Paragraph 3.1:

    [ ] day care: $ _____ to _____;
    [ ] educational expenses: $ _____ to _____;
    [ ] long distance transportation: $_____to _____
    _____.
    [ ] other:

3.13 PERIODIC MODIFICATION.

[ ] Does not apply.
[ ] Child support shall be adjusted periodically as follows:

3.14 INCOME TAX EXEMPTIONS.

[ ] Does not apply.
[ ] Tax exemptions for the children shall be allocated as follows:

[ ] The parents shall sign the federal income tax dependency exemption waiver.

ORDER OF CHILD SUPPORT
RCW 26.09.175; 26.26.132(5)
Page 8

2   3.15   MEDICAL INSURANCE.

4   Health insurance coverage for the child(ren) listed in Paragraph 3.1 shall be provided by the [ ] mother [ ] father [ ] both parents if coverage that can
6   be extended to cover the child(ren) is or becomes available through employment or is union related and the cost of such coverage does not
8   exceed $ _____(twenty-five percent of the obligated parent's basic child support obligation).

10

     [ ]   Health insurance coverage shall be provided as set forth above by the
12   [ ] mother [ ] father [ ] both parents, even if the cost of such coverage exceeds 25% of the obligated parent's basic child support
14   obligation.

     [ ]   The reasons for not ordering the [ ] mother [ ] father to provide
16   health insurance coverage for the child(ren) are:

18

20   The parents shall maintain health insurance coverage, as set forth in paragraph 3.1, if available, until further order of the court or until health insurance is no longer available through the parents' employer or union and
22   no conversion privileges exist to continue coverage following termination of employment.

24

26   A parent who is required under this order to provide health insurance coverage is liable for any covered health care costs for which that parent receives direct payment from an insurer.

28

30   A parent who is required under this order to provide health insurance coverage shall provide proof of such coverage within twenty days of the entry of this order or within twenty days of the date such coverage becomes
32   available, to:

34   [ ]   the physical custodian.

     [ ]   the Washington State Support Registry if the parent has been notified
36   or ordered to make payments to the Washington State Support Registry.

38

40   If proof of health insurance coverage is not provided within twenty days the obligee or the Department of Social and Health Services may seek direct enforcement of the coverage through the obligor's employer or union without
42   further notice to the obligor as provided under Chapter 26.18 RCW.

2 3.16 EXTRAORDINARY HEALTH CARE EXPENSES.

4 The OBLIGOR shall pay _____% of extraordinary health care expenses (the obligor's proportional share of income from the Support Schedule
6 Worksheet A, line 6), if monthly medical expenses exceed $ _____ per child (5% of the basic support obligation from Worksheet A, line 5).

8

3.17 BACK CHILD SUPPORT.
10

[ ]   Does not apply.
12 [ ]   The obligee parent is awarded a judgment against the obligor parent in the amount of $ _____ for back child support for
14 the period from _____ to _____.
                              (Date)   (Date)
16

3.18 OTHER.
18

20

22

24

26

Dated: _____   _____
28   Judge/Commissioner

30 Presented by: Approved for entry:
                                               Notice of presentation waived:
32

34 _____   _____
Signature and Washington State Bar   Signature and Washington State Bar
36 Number, if applicable   Number, if applicable

38 I apply for full support enforcement services.

40 _____
Signature of Party
42

ORDER OF CHILD SUPPORT
RCW 26.09.175; 26.26.132(5)
Page 10

SELF-COUNSEL PRESS
1704 N. State Street
Bellingham, Washington 98225
FORM USA-D-WASH (11-10)92

IN THE SUPERIOR COURT OF THE STATE OF WASHINGTON,
COUNTY OF _____

In re the Marriage of:

No._____

_____
PETITIONER

- and -

_____
RESPONDENT

}
}
}
}
}
}
}
}

Declaration of Non-Military Service

STATE OF WASHINGTON

COUNTY OF _____

}
}
}

ss.

_____, declares under penalty of perjury under the laws of the state of Washington that the following is true:

I am the Petitioner, above named. I am the spouse of _____, who is the Respondent, above named. I know of my own personal knowledge that the Respondent is not in the military service of the United States. This declaration is made in connection with the entry of a Decree of Dissolution in the above-entitled proceeding and is made pursuant to the provisions of the Soldiers and Sailors' Civil Relief Act of March 4, 1918, as amended.

_____
Petitioner, In Person

SELF-COUNSEL PRESS INC.
1704 N. State Street
Bellingham, Washington 98225
FORM USA-D-WASH (5-1)90

IN THE SUPERIOR COURT OF THE STATE OF WASHINGTON,
COUNTY OF _____

In re the Marriage of:

No._____

}
}
_____ }
PETITIONER }   **Declaration of**
- and - }   **Non-Military Service**
}
_____ }
RESPONDENT }

STATE OF WASHINGTON   }
COUNTY OF _____ }   ss.

_____, declares under penalty of perjury under the laws
of the state of Washington that the following is true:

I am the Petitioner, above named. I am the spouse of _____,
who is the Respondent, above named. I know of my own personal knowledge that
the Respondent is not in the military service of the United States. This declaration
is made in connection with the entry of a Decree of Dissolution in the above-entitled
proceeding and is made pursuant to the provisions of the Soldiers and Sailors' Civil
Relief Act of March 4, 1918, as amended.

_____
Petitioner, In Person

SELF-COUNSEL PRESS INC.
1704 N. State Street
Bellingham, Washington 98225
FORM USA-D-WASH (5-1)90

IN THE SUPERIOR COURT OF THE STATE OF WASHINGTON
COUNTY OF _____

In re the Marriage of:

No._____

_____   }
                                    }   **Waiver of Rights**
PETITIONER   }   **Under Soldiers and**
- and -   }   **Sailors' Civil Relief**
                                    }
_____   }   **Act and Admission of**
RESPONDENT   }   **Service**

My name is_____ and I am the above-named Respondent. My spouse has petitioned the above-entitled court to terminate our marriage under the laws of the state of Washington. I am a member of the United States military service and I am informed of my rights under the Soldiers and Sailors' Civil Relief Act of March 4, 1918, as amended. I do hereby waive my rights under the Soldiers and Sailors' Civil Relief Act and I request the court to terminate our marriage as requested by the Petitioner.

I received a copy of the Summons and Petition in this matter as issued by the court under the above case number on the _____day of_____ , 19____.

I admit and acknowledge service of process upon me in this matter.

_____
(signature)

Name: _____

Rank: _____

Serial Number: _____

Unit: _____

Subscribed and sworn to before me this_____day of_____, 19____ .

_____
Judge Advocate

WAIVER OF RIGHTS UNDER SOLDIERS AND
SAILORS' CIVIL RELIEF ACT AND ADMISSION

SELF-COUNSEL PRESS INC
1704 N. State Street
Bellingham, Washington 98225
FORM USA-D-WASH (6-1)90

SUPERIOR COURT OF WASHINGTON FOR SNOHOMISH COUNTY

In Re the Marriage Of:)
)   (No Mandatory Form Developed)
)
)
)   No.
                     Petitioner,   )
)
and   )
)   CALENDAR NOTE: Must be filed with Clerk not later than
)   six (6) working days preceding date noted. (DO NOT note
)   on both Presiding and Commissioner Calendars at the same
                     Respondent.   )   time.)

TO: The Clerk of the Court:

PRESIDING DEPT.--   Date:_____

_____   ONLY those civil matters not listed for Commissioner   Tues. thru Fri. at 10:00 a.m.
         Depts below, plus all motions regarding trial dates.

         (Adoptions, Reasonableness Hearings and Minor   Nature of Hearing:
         Settlements are specially set through P.J. Law clerk:
         388-3421.)   _____

COMMISSIONER DEPTS--

_____   CIVIL CALENDAR   Date:_____
         Defaults, Discovery Motions & enforcement thereof;   Tues. thru Fri. at 10:00 a.m.
         Supplemental Proceedings; Unlawful Detainer, Probate   Nature of Hearing:
         Guardianship & Receivership actions; Motion to Amend
         Pleadings.
                                                          _____

__XX__   FAMILY LAW/DOMESTIC CALENDAR   Date:_____
         (Except matters relating to trial dates and trial   Mon,Tues,Thu,Fri: 9:30 a.m. _____
         continuances.) Counsel must indicate specific   OR Mon. thru Fri. 1:30 p.m. _____
         calendar at right   Nature of Hearing:

                                                          _____

_____   PRO SE DISSOLUTION CALENDAR   Date:_____
                                                          Wednesday at 10:00 a.m.

I hereby certify that I mailed a copy of this document to the
attorneys/parties listed hereon, postage prepaid, on the _____
day of _____,1992.

Attorneys and addresses: Noted by:

                                _____

                                Attorney for

SELF-COUNSEL PRESS
1704 N. State Street
Bellingham, Washington 98225
FORM USA-D-WASH (12-1)92

IN THE SUPERIOR COURT OF THE STATE OF WASHINGTON
COUNTY OF _____

In re the Marriage of:

No. _____

_____ }

_____ }

PETITIONER } **Motion and**

} **Declaration for Order**

- and - } **to Commence and**

} **Prosecute Proceeding**

_____ } **In Forma Pauperis**

RESPONDENT }

_____ }

STATE OF WASHINGTON } ss.

COUNTY OF _____ }

_____, declares under penalty of perjury under the laws of the state of Washington that the following is true:

I.

I am one of the parties in the above-entitled proceeding. My marriage to_____ _____is irretrievably broken. We are at this time unable to live together as married persons. This proceeding to terminate our marriage is brought in good faith and it is my present intention to proceed to a final dissolution of our marriage.

II.

I bring this proceeding in person, without an attorney, because I lack financial means to pay legal counsel. I cannot, without financial hardship, pay to the clerk of this court the statutory fee for filing my Petition.

SELF-COUNSEL PRESS
1704 N. State Street
Bellingham, Washington 98225
FORM USA-D-WASH (13-1)90

WHEREFORE, I request the court for:

(1) ☐ An order allowing commencement and prosecution of this proceeding
In Forma Pauperis;

(2) ☐ An order directing the clerk of this court to file and issue my Petition or
any other papers herein without any fee, cost or charge whatsoever;

(3) ☐ An order of this court authorizing me to serve the Summons and
Petition upon my spouse by certified mail with return receipt, deposited
with the court at the time of the final hearing herein.

_____
(petitioner's signature)

SELF-COUNSEL PRESS
1704 N. State Street
Bellingham, Washington 98225
FORM USA-D-WASH (13-2)90

IN THE SUPERIOR COURT OF THE STATE OF WASHINGTON
COUNTY OF _____

In re the Marriage of:

No. _____

_____
PETITIONER

- and -

_____
RESPONDENT

}
}
}
}
}
}
}

Order Authorizing Proceeding In Forma Pauperis

The Petitioner, above named, having presented to the court a sufficient affidavit and declaration to proceed In Forma Pauperis and the court being of the opinion that the order asked for should issue, now therefore, it is:

☐ ORDERED, ADJUDGED, and DECREED that the parties are hereby authorized to prosecute this action In Forma Pauperis; and the clerk of this court is ordered and directed to file and issue papers and pleadings as requested by either party without prepayment of any fee, cost or charge whatsoever. In approving this order, the court reserves the right to review this authorization and require the payment of the fee if justified at the time of final hearing.

☐ It is further ORDERED, ADJUDGED, and DECREED that the Petitioner, herein, is authorized to serve the Summons and Petition, herein, on the Respondent by certified mail with the post office return receipt deposited with the court at the time of the final hearing herein.

Done in open Court this_____day of _____, 19 ___.

_____
Judge/Court Commissioner

Presented by:

_____

In Person

SELF-COUNSEL PRESS INC.
1704 N. State Street
Bellingham, Washington 98225
FORM USA-D-WASH (14-1)90